THE GREEN BARBECUE

FOR PADMINI,
SOME ALTERNATIVES
TO POTATO SALAD FOR YOU

THE GREEN BARBECUE

VEGAN & VEGETARIAN
RECIPES TO COOK OUTDOORS & IN

RUKMINI IYER

Countryman Press

An Imprint of W. W. Norton & Company
Independent Publishers Since 1923

CONTENTS

> INTRODUCTION 6

> SOMETHING TO START 17

> FRESH & LIGHT 45

> SOMETHING SUBSTANTIAL 73

> TAKE IT TO THE BEACH (OR PARK) 163

> SOMETHING SWEET 193

> WHAT TO DO WITH YOUR LEFTOVERS 215

> ACKNOWLEDGMENTS 223

> INDEX 224

INTRODUCTION

I'm not sure there's anything nicer than cooking and eating outside. With good company, perhaps a dog or two, or even just contemplatively cooking a dish for yourself, it's incredibly satisfying to break cooking down into its most simple components: one heat source and a bit of food. I'll often add a chopping board on a patio table to maximize my time outside with minimal fuss and as much enjoyment as anyone could expect from a bit of lazy food prep in the sunshine— lunch or dinner rolling off the grill in courses, with nothing more from you than occasionally flipping something on the barbecue, drink in hand. As a certified oven-and-stovetop enthusiast, in many cases I've provided alternative indoor cooking instructions in case you encounter bad weather, live in an apartment where barbecuing isn't practical, or feel like making the dishes at a colder time of the year.

Why a vegetarian book? As readers of *The Green Roasting Tin* will know, my family is vegetarian, and over the past few years most of my close friends have become vegetarian too. I myself eat meat very rarely, and it's the combination of flavors and textures in plant-based cooking that are of real interest, as that's what I cook for the people closest to me. The idea of an entirely vegetarian or vegan feast, packed with texture, flavor, and color, which opens up the world of cooking and eating outdoors to the people I love, is immensely appealing since barbecues are almost exclusively associated with carnivorous cooking—though this is something that is happily changing. I must namecheck one of my food mentors, Genevieve Taylor, whose vegetarian barbecue book, *Charred,* I have been dying to read but refrained from doing so while writing this book so as not to inadvertently cross over with the content here. She is the queen of cooking outdoors—buy both books and double the number of vegetarian dishes for your barbecue.

Whether you're vegetarian—or indeed vegan, as more than half the recipes in this book turned out vegan almost by accident—or cooking for vegetarian and vegan friends, I hope this book will give you lots of ideas to maximize your time cooking and eating outdoors throughout the summer.

ABOUT YOUR BARBECUE

GAS OR CHARCOAL?

I have spent the past couple of summers (and one memorable winter—who says you can't barbecue in the snow?) cooking outside with a variety of barbecues. Expensive gas range? Check (although sadly not mine). Inexpensive little gas barbecue (which took hours to attach to the gas canister in the pouring rain)? You bet.

And then charcoal—the messiest, most unpredictable, and my favorite. (Although I wish people would tell me when I've managed to smudge coal on my nose like an extra from *Mary Poppins*.) From setups not very much more complex than a metal bucket covered with a grill, which you'll see pictured in these pages, to a rather nicer Weber, a smart tabletop Hestan, and my much-loved little Prakti stove, most of the recipes in this book have been tested on a variety of different charcoal grills. My thoughts—which are entirely subjective—are as follows:

Gas: Couldn't be easier. The temperature of the grill will be stable throughout, and the grill will have a top, so it will be as controlled as cooking indoors. Downside: You'll lose the smokiness and primal fire factor of cooking over charcoal or wood.

Charcoal: Pleasing caveperson + fire factor. The smoke will impart an incredible flavor to the food. You can use seasoned wood or dry garden sticks on the fire (eucalyptus, apple, and plum are particularly nice) for extra flavor, or branches of rosemary, lavender, or thyme. Lots of vegetables (beets, eggplants, potatoes, sweet potatoes) can go directly on the coals to cook, and more delicate things (tomatoes, feta, marinated black beans) can go on the coals in foil packets. Downsides: The temperature will vary through the lifetime of the coal, and until you get a feel for cooking on it (see page 11) there's a risk your food will burn before it's cooked through or just sit there getting smoked but not cooking at all. But I'd still rather try on charcoal than not.

Tips for Charcoal: Use natural fire starters or a few twists of newspaper to get your coals going. Remember: You need a decent airflow, so don't pack your coals too tightly in the barbecue. Once your charcoal starts turning white around the edges—if it's good coal (see below)—and the flames have died down, it's kicking off enough heat to start cooking something gently, so make the most of the heat and start cooking within 10 minutes of lighting it. Your coals are at their hottest when glowing white, and if that is going to be too fierce for whatever you're cooking, use something suitably long-handled to bank them up on one side—this will be the hotter end, and you can cook more delicate food on the cooler side.

Note on Charcoal: Please try to avoid gas station charcoal and buy the best charcoal sustainably made in the United States, which is a purer product—better for you and for the environment.

Lids: If your barbecue doesn't have one, I recommend using a deep, inverted metal roasting pan instead; just be careful taking it on and off, and use heat-proof gloves.

USEFUL THINGS TO HAVE

YOUR MINIMALIST OUTDOOR COOKING TOOLS CHECKLIST:

GAS OR CHARCOAL BARBECUE + HEAT SOURCE

LONG-HANDLED TONGS
(and you only need one as—hooray!—everything is vegetarian)

LONG-HANDLED METAL FLIPPER

SMALL BOWL FOR OLIVE OIL

HEATPROOF (IDEALLY SILICONE) BRUSH to brush food with olive oil

COUPLE OF BOWLS OR ROASTING PANS to put cooked food in

BIG TRAY to put all of the above on

SLIGHTLY MORE MAXIMALIST IF PREPPING OUTDOORS:

CHOPPING BOARD

KNIFE AND SPEED PEELER

COUPLE OF BOWLS for prepped food and vegetable peelings/scraps

AND IF YOU'RE GOING ON A PICNIC:

PAPER TOWELS, lots of paper towels

SOMETHING TO SIT ON, EAT FROM, AND DRINK OUT OF

WINE, WATER, SPARKLING WATER

ANTIBACTERIAL WIPES

OLD SHOPPING BAGS to put trash in

SOMETHING TO START

SERVE PILED ON A PLATTER
OR HAND AROUND WITH DRINKS.

SOMETHING TO START

ROSEMARY GRILLED MUSHROOMS
WITH CRISPY HALLOUMI & LEMON   20

SPICED CHARRED BABY CARROTS
WITH HAZELNUTS & DILL (VEGAN)   22

GRILLED CHERRIES WITH WARM GOAT CHEESE,
MINT & WALNUTS   26

CHARRED ASPARAGUS
WITH CHILI, PEANUTS & COCONUT (VEGAN)   28

GRILLED PINEAPPLE, HALLOUMI
& MINT SKEWERS   30

JERK CAULIFLOWER WINGS
WITH BLUE CHEESE DIP   32

GRILLED WATERMELON
WITH FETA, CUCUMBER & MINT   34

SPICED PANEER KOFTE
WITH YOGURT & CILANTRO   36

CRISPY GNOCCHI—ON A SKEWER—
WITH CHARRED BELL PEPPERS
& BASIL PESTO (VEGAN)   40

FETA & ALMOND–STUFFED
PADRÓN PEPPERS   42

ROSEMARY GRILLED MUSHROOMS WITH CRISPY HALLOUMI & LEMON

I had intended to use rosemary branches as skewers for this dish, but this left me grumbling in the kitchen with crumbled halloumi and rather crushed—if fragrant—herbs. Make your life easier and use storebought skewers, chopping the rosemary for a marinade instead—less hassle, equally delicious.

Serves: 4
Prep: 15 minutes
Cook: 10 minutes

14 ounces (400 g) baby button
   mushrooms
9 ounces (250 g) good halloumi
   cheese, cut into ¾-inch (2 cm)
   chunks
2 tablespoons chopped
   fresh rosemary
2 tablespoons olive oil
8 or so skewers, soaked if wooden

FOR THE DRESSING
2 tablespoons extra virgin olive oil
1 lemon, zest and juice
1 tablespoon chopped
   fresh rosemary
1 teaspoon freshly ground
   black pepper

Gently stir the mushrooms, halloumi, rosemary, and olive oil together in a large bowl. Thread the mushrooms and halloumi alternately onto the skewers, working carefully so as not to break up the cheese.

Whisk together the extra virgin olive oil, lemon zest and juice, rosemary, and black pepper, and set aside.

Once your barbecue is good and hot, grill the skewers for 4–5 minutes on each side, until the cheese is nicely browned and the mushrooms are cooked through.

Arrange the skewers on a platter, pour the dressing on top, and serve hot.

Note: If you can't get baby button mushrooms, use halved ordinary button mushrooms. You want the mushrooms a similar size to the halloumi, so quarter them if they're very large.

SPICED CHARRED BABY CARROTS WITH HAZELNUTS & DILL

These spiced carrots are ridiculously moreish, to the extent that I've had to double up the recipe. Crushing your spices whole with a mortar and pestle makes all the difference to the flavor (I've been known to improvise by chopping them with a sharp knife instead)—worth trying if you have whole spices in your kitchen already; or, you can just use the already–ground versions.

Serves: 4
Prep: 10 minutes
Cook: 25 minutes

10½ ounces (300 g) baby carrots
   or small peeled carrots
1 heaped teaspoon coriander seeds
1 teaspoon cumin seeds
1 teaspoon smoked paprika
1 tablespoon olive oil
½ teaspoon sea salt flakes

FOR THE DRESSING
1 tablespoon olive oil
1 tablespoon maple syrup
½ lemon, juice only
A pinch of sea salt flakes
⅓ ounce (10 g) fresh dill, roughly
   chopped
1 ounce (30 g) hazelnuts, roughly
   chopped

Parboil the carrots for 5 minutes to give them a head start, then drain well.

Bash the coriander and cumin seeds with a mortar and pestle until coarsely ground, then add to a bowl with the carrots, smoked paprika, olive oil, and sea salt. Stir gently to coat.

For the dressing, mix the olive oil, maple syrup, lemon juice, sea salt, dill, and hazelnuts together. Taste, adjust the seasoning as needed, and set aside.

Once your barbecue is medium hot, cook the carrots for 6–8 minutes per side, until just starting to color. You want them lightly charred and cooked through, so keep an eye on them and move them around as needed.

Once the carrots are cooked, place them on a platter and pour the hazelnut dressing on top. Serve hot.

Note: If you don't have maple syrup and you aren't vegan, you can use honey instead.

GRILLED CHERRIES
WITH WARM GOAT CHEESE, MINT & WALNUTS

In this dish, you heat the cherries on the barbecue before tumbling them over warm goat cheese with fresh mint and crumbled walnuts—an easy, elegant, five-ingredient starter.

Serves: 4
Prep: 10 minutes
Cook: 15 minutes

7 ounces (200 g) fresh cherries, whole
5 ounces (150 g) goat cheese log with a rind
2 tablespoons chopped walnuts
2 tablespoons chopped fresh mint
2 tablespoons extra virgin olive oil

Place the cherries in the center of a large piece of foil, then wrap it into a neat, sealed parcel with the seam along the top. Place the foil packet directly on the coals (or on the grill if using a gas barbecue) and cook for 10–15 minutes, until the cherries are softened—they'll steam inside the packet.

Just before the cherries are done, place the goat cheese log on the barbecue for 3–4 minutes, turning it every minute or so, just to warm it through. (The rind will protect it from the heat; don't try this if your cheese doesn't have one.)

Cut the warm goat cheese into four equal pieces and arrange them on your serving plates. Divide the hot cherries between the plates, then scatter the walnuts and mint on top. Drizzle the cherry juice from the foil packet and the extra virgin olive oil, and serve hot.

Cook indoors: Put the foil packet into the oven for 15 minutes at 400°F (200°C).

CHARRED ASPARAGUS
WITH CHILI, PEANUTS & COCONUT

Good, seasonal asparagus requires little more than butter, salt, and lemon juice—but if you feel like changing it up, I love this lightly spiced version. The crunchy peanut and coconut work beautifully with the charred asparagus.

Serves: 4
Prep: 10 minutes
Cook: 10 minutes

1.1 pounds (500 g) asparagus
    spears, trimmed
1 tablespoon olive oil
A pinch of sea salt flakes

FOR THE DRESSING
1¾ ounces (50 g) salted peanuts
1 fresh red chili,
    roughly chopped
1 teaspoon sea salt flakes
1¾ ounces (50 g) unsweetened
    shredded coconut
2 tablespoons olive or neutral oil
1 lime, juice only

Toss the asparagus spears, olive oil, and sea salt flakes in a large bowl and set aside.

Put the peanuts, chili, and sea salt flakes in a mortar, then roughly pound them together with a pestle until well broken down. Stir in the coconut, oil, and lime juice, then taste and adjust the salt as needed.

Alternatively, if you don't have a mortar and pestle, finely chop the peanuts and chili, then combine with the other dressing ingredients.

Once your barbecue is good and hot, cook the asparagus for 3–4 minutes per side, until just charred and cooked through. Put the spears back into their bowl with the peanut and lime dressing, give them a good shake to get them well coated, then transfer to a serving platter and eat immediately, ideally with your fingers.

GRILLED PINEAPPLE, HALLOUMI & MINT SKEWERS

The Flavor Thesaurus advises readers to "outsnoot the snobs" who disapprove of cheese and pineapple on a stick—they have complementary flavor compounds that make them a scientifically excellent match as well as a nostalgic one. These skewers are an update on the classic and the perfect way to kick off a summer party (for grown-ups).

Makes: 5 large skewers
Prep: 15 minutes
Cook: under 15 minutes

1 medium pineapple, peeled, cored,
    and cut into 1-inch (2½ cm) pieces
8–9 ounces (225–250 g) halloumi,
    cut into 1-inch (2½ cm) cubes
1 fresh red chili, thinly sliced
¾ ounce (20 g) fresh mint, finely
    chopped
1 lime, juice only
Olive oil, for brushing
5 skewers, soaked if wooden

Combine the pineapple and halloumi in a large bowl. Mix the chili, mint, and lime juice in another bowl, then pour half the mixture over the pineapple and halloumi, and gently stir.

If you have time, leave the pineapple and halloumi to sit for 15 minutes. If not, alternately skewer the fruit and cheese onto long wooden or metal skewers.

Once your barbecue is ready, grill the skewers for about 5–7 minutes on each side. You can brush the pineapple pieces with the oil if they start to look dry. Don't try to flip the skewers too quickly or the halloumi will stick to the barbecue.

Once the fruit and cheese are nicely charred on both sides, remove to a serving platter, drizzle with the remaining chili, lime, and mint dressing, and serve hot.

Note: Cut the halloumi on the larger side or it'll fall to bits when you try to skewer it. This recipe can be doubled or tripled as needed, or you can make it go a little further by dividing the amount above between 10 skewers rather than 5.

JERK CAULIFLOWER WINGS
WITH BLUE CHEESE DIP

An easy, delicious snack to hand around with drinks. I'd be tempted to double up on the dip and use it the next day in sandwiches.

Serves: 4 as a snack
Prep: 10 minutes
Cook: 10 minutes

1 large cauliflower
2 tablespoons olive oil
1½ tablespoons jerk seasoning
1 teaspoon sea salt flakes

FOR THE DIP
3½ ounces (100 g) blue cheese, crumbled
3½ ounces (100 g) natural yogurt
1 ounce (30g) mayonnaise
Freshly ground black pepper

Cut the cauliflower into medium florets, then put them into a large bowl with the olive oil, jerk seasoning, and sea salt flakes. Mix well to coat, then set aside.

For the dip, stir the blue cheese, yogurt, and mayonnaise together with the freshly ground black pepper.

Once your barbecue is good and hot, grill the cauliflower for 4–5 minutes per side, until charred and cooked through.

Scatter the florets with a little more salt as needed and serve hot with the dip on the side.

GRILLED WATERMELON
WITH FETA, CUCUMBER & MINT

A light, refreshing dish—perfect as a palate cleanser before moving on to the next round. Use your favorite type of melon—watermelon works well, but cantaloupe or Galia are just as nice.

Serves: 6
Prep: 15 minutes
Cook: 15 minutes

1 small watermelon, quartered
   and cut into ½-inch (1½ cm) slices
Olive oil, for brushing
9 ounces (250 g) feta
½ cucumber, halved and thinly
   sliced

FOR THE DRESSING
2 tablespoons olive oil
½ lemon, juice only
A large handful of fresh mint,
   roughly chopped
1 teaspoon fennel seeds (optional)

Once your barbecue is good and hot, brush the watermelon slices with a little olive oil and barbecue for 3–4 minutes on each side, until just charred.

If you're using a charcoal barbecue, wrap the feta in foil and place directly on the coals for 5 minutes per side to warm through. Alternatively, place the foil packet on the grill for the same amount of time.

Mix the olive oil, lemon juice, mint, and fennel seeds (if using) together. Once the watermelon is cooked, arrange it on a large platter. Scatter the cucumber over it along with the feta, crumbled into large pieces. Drizzle with the mint dressing and serve warm.

SPICED PANEER KOFTE
WITH YOGURT & CILANTRO

These kofte are so addictive that I'm surprised they're legal: a crisp, just-charred exterior, meltingly soft inside, and perfectly spiced. It's well worth doubling up the quantities on this recipe because—among four—a platter of these will disappear very, very quickly.

Serves: 4
Prep: 20 minutes
             + 1 hour chilling
Cook: 10 minutes

One 8-ounce (225 g) block paneer, grated
3½ ounces (100 g) cold cooked potato, mashed
1 ounce (30 g) fresh cilantro, chopped
1 teaspoon sea salt flakes
1 teaspoon ground cumin
1 teaspoon ground coriander
½ teaspoon ground turmeric
½ teaspoon chili powder
1 teaspoon freshly ground black pepper
3 fresh curry leaves, chopped (optional)
1 tablespoon olive or neutral oil, plus more for brushing
1 free-range egg yolk
Natural yogurt and lime wedges, to serve

Mix all the ingredients, except the yogurt and lime, in a large bowl until thoroughly combined. Taste and adjust the seasoning as necessary, then using your hands, press the mixture into small oval kebab shapes as pictured—squeeze them really well so they compress, as this will help them stay together when cooking. Chill the kebabs in the fridge for at least an hour or overnight.

When you're ready to cook, wait until the barbecue is good and hot, then generously oil the grill—this will help prevent the kebabs from sticking. Grill the kebabs for 8–10 minutes, turning them gently every couple of minutes, until golden brown and crisp all over.

Serve as soon as they come off the barbecue with yogurt and lime wedges alongside.

Cook indoors: Bake for 15–20 minutes at 400°F (200°C) before finishing them off under a hot broiler.

CRISPY GNOCCHI—ON A SKEWER—WITH CHARRED BELL PEPPERS & BASIL PESTO

Could I write a book without featuring crispy gnocchi? Of course not. So I give you my proudest barbecue creation. Forget about threading just plain old vegetables on a stick—here, you intersperse veggies of your choice (I've done bell peppers here, but see the note below) on skewers with just-blanched gnocchi. The result is crisp perfection like you wouldn't believe.

Serves: 3–4
Prep: 15 minutes
Cook: under 10 minutes

One 1.1-pound (500 g) package
   gnocchi
3 mixed bell peppers, chopped
   into gnocchi-size pieces
   (don't use green peppers)
2 tablespoons vegan basil pesto
3 tablespoons olive oil,
   plus more for brushing
A pinch of sea salt flakes
A good amount of freshly
   ground black pepper
8–12 skewers, soaked if wooden

FOR THE DRESSING
½ lemon, juice only
4 tablespoons vegan basil pesto
2 tablespoons extra virgin olive oil
A pinch of sea salt flakes

Place the gnocchi into a bowl of just-boiled water and leave to blanch for 2 minutes, then drain and run under cold water to cool.

Put the gnocchi into a large bowl with the chopped bell peppers, vegan basil pesto, olive oil, sea salt flakes, and freshly ground black pepper, and mix well to coat. At this point you could refrigerate the gnocchi until you're ready to barbecue.

Thread the gnocchi and pepper alternately onto the skewers. Once your barbecue is good and hot, brush one side of the skewers with oil, then lay them over the barbecue at a slight angle (this stops them from falling through) and cook for 4–5 minutes, until the gnocchi are crisp and brown. Brush the tops with oil, then turn over and repeat with the other side.

Meanwhile, mix the lemon juice, pesto, and extra virgin olive oil with a pinch of sea salt flakes to taste. Once the skewers are cooked through, serve immediately with the basil dressing.

Note: There's really no limit to the number of things you could pair with gnocchi on a stick: try cherry tomatoes and halloumi or tofu, or cubes of fresh fennel and halved figs. And you could use red pesto, harissa, or mustard mixed with olive oil as a marinade.

FETA & ALMOND–STUFFED PADRÓN PEPPERS

I love ordering Padrón peppers on the basis that "some are hot, the others are not" (sounds better in Spanish)—although I have yet to come across a truly spicy one. While there's nothing like a round of barbecued peppers just by themselves, scattered with crunchy salt, these little numbers, each stuffed with feta and a plump almond, are a wonderful treat with drinks.

Serves: 4
Prep: 15 minutes
Cook: under 15 minutes

9 ounces (250 g) Padrón peppers
5 ounces (150 g) feta cheese,
  roughly chopped
A handful of unsalted
  blanched almonds
Olive oil, to drizzle

Slice each pepper on one side, making sure not to cut all the way through. Stuff with a little feta—enough to fill the pepper but still allow it to close up nicely—and add an almond. Repeat until you've prepped all the peppers. At this stage they can be refrigerated until you're ready to barbecue.

Once your barbecue is good and hot, drizzle the peppers with a little olive oil, then transfer them to the barbecue. Leave them for 3–4 minutes, until puffed up and blackened, then flip them over and cook on the other side for a further 2–3 minutes to finish.

Serve immediately with drinks (and a warning in case someone gets the mythical hot pepper).

Note: You could definitely do this dish with the colorful packets of mini bell peppers, but allow for a little more feta, as they tend to be larger than Padrón peppers.

FRESH & LIGHT

THE PERFECT COMBINATION OF GRILLED AND CHARRED VEGETABLES COOKED ON THE BARBECUE, WITH FRESH LEAVES, HERBS, SALADY BITS, AND PUNCHY DRESSINGS.

PICK ONE OR TWO AS PART OF A SHARING FEAST FOR A VARIETY OF TEXTURES, COLORS, AND FLAVORS.

FRESH & LIGHT

GRILLED ASPARAGUS, RADISHES & BURRATA
WITH LEMON & BASIL   48

CARAMELIZED MANGO WITH SMASHED CUCUMBER,
PEANUTS & LIME (VEGAN)   50

HALLOUMI WITH RED PEPPERS, ARTICHOKES
& PRESERVED LEMON   52

GRAPEFRUIT & FENNEL PANZANELLA
WITH HONEY & WATERCRESS   54

CHARRED BROCCOLINI
WITH ORANGES, BLUE CHEESE & WALNUTS   56

GRILLED ZUCCHINI
WITH PARMESAN, ALMONDS & LEMON   58

GRILLED PAPAYA
WITH TAMARIND, CHILI & COCONUT (VEGAN)   60

SUNSHINE SALAD: GRILLED GRAPEFRUIT & AVOCADO
WITH ARUGULA & POMEGRANATE (VEGAN)   62

SRI LANKAN–STYLE EGGPLANT SKEWERS
& PICKLED RED ONION (VEGAN)   64

BLACKENED PEPPERS WITH WALNUTS, CHILI
& FENNEL SEEDS (VEGAN)   68

THYME-ROASTED CHERRY TOMATOES
WITH CORIANDER SEEDS & MOZZARELLA   70

GRILLED ASPARAGUS, RADISHES & BURRATA WITH LEMON & BASIL

I love the combination of crisp and barbecued radishes with the grilled asparagus, burrata, and the crunch of good sea salt flakes. All this needs is a simple lemon and basil dressing, and you have a sharing platter that is both moreish and beautiful.

Serves: 4
Prep: 10 minutes
Cook: under 15 minutes

14 ounces (400 g) asparagus
   spears
7 ounces (200 g) radishes, half of
   them halved, the rest very thinly
   sliced (see note)
2 tablespoons olive oil
A pinch of sea salt flakes
1 burrata (about 5 ounces [150 g]
   drained), at room temperature
A handful of fresh basil leaves, torn

FOR THE DRESSING
3 tablespoons extra virgin olive oil
1 lemon, juice only
Sea salt flakes
Freshly ground black pepper

Trim the ends of the asparagus spears (or snap the ends off at the point where they break easily), then put them in a large bowl with the halved radishes, olive oil, and a pinch of sea salt, and mix well.

Put the thinly sliced radishes into cold water to crisp up. In a separate bowl, mix the extra virgin olive oil, lemon juice, a big pinch of sea salt flakes, and freshly ground black pepper for the dressing. Taste and adjust the salt as needed.

Once your barbecue is ready, grill the asparagus and halved radishes for about 6–8 minutes, turning them every so often, until nicely charred.

Transfer to a serving platter, scatter the drained sliced radishes on top, and drizzle with most of the lemon dressing. Place the burrata in the middle of the dish and pour the remaining dressing over it, then sprinkle with the basil leaves and serve hot or at room temperature.

Note: To prepare the radishes, halve the smallest ones and slice the largest ones to make sure you don't lose any through the barbecue grill.

CARAMELIZED MANGO
WITH SMASHED CUCUMBER, PEANUTS & LIME

This dish is fresh, light, and everything you'd want from a grazing plate on a hot summer day. As a bonus, smashing cucumbers is very therapeutic.

Serves: 4
Prep: 15 minutes
Cook: 15 minutes

2 just underripe mangoes
1 tablespoon olive oil
1 tablespoon sugar
½ cucumber
¾ ounce (20 g) fresh mint leaves
1 fresh red chili, finely chopped
1 teaspoon sea salt flakes
1 lime, zest and juice
1 tablespoon olive or neutral oil
A handful of salted peanuts,
  roughly chopped

Cut the "cheeks" off the mangoes, then halve each one so you have four quarters from each mango.

Once your barbecue is good and hot, brush the cut sides of the mangoes with the olive oil and sprinkle with a little sugar, then barbecue for 4–5 minutes per cut side, until you get nice caramelized char marks.

Meanwhile, cut the cucumber into 1½-inch (4 cm) logs. Pop them into a sturdy plastic bag, squeeze out the air, then give them a good beating with a rolling pin to roughly break them up.

Mix the smashed cucumber with the mint, chili, sea salt flakes, lime juice, and oil, then adjust the seasoning to taste.

Once the mango is cooked, arrange the pieces on a serving platter with the cucumber, drizzle any remaining dressing over the mango, sprinkle with the chopped peanuts, and serve hot or at room temperature.

Note: You can gnaw the flesh off the mango pits so as not to waste it—just don't go near where the stem meets the pit. It provides a similar sensation to eating kiwi when one is mildly allergic.

HALLOUMI WITH RED PEPPERS, ARTICHOKES & PRESERVED LEMON

Summer on a plate. After returning from Morocco, I started putting preserved lemons into everything—they work beautifully with the red peppers in this dish.

Serves: 6
Prep: 10 minutes
Cook: 20 minutes

6 pointy red peppers
A handful of fresh thyme
6 garlic cloves
1 tablespoon olive oil
9 ounces (250 g) manouri, kefalotyri, or halloumi cheese, sliced

FOR THE MARINATED ARTICHOKES
1 preserved lemon, finely chopped
1 lemon, juice only
One 10-ounce (280 g) jar sliced artichokes, drained
2 tablespoons oil from the artichoke jar
A handful of fresh thyme leaves

Make a cut down the side of each pepper and carefully stuff each one with a few thyme sprigs and a garlic clove.

To make the marinated artichokes, rinse the chopped preserved lemon well in a sieve (there's plenty of salt from the cheese, so you want to remove some of the brine). Mix with the lemon juice, sliced artichokes, artichoke oil, and thyme leaves and set aside.

Once your barbecue is medium hot, rub the peppers with the olive oil and barbecue for 3–5 minutes per side before covering with a lid or an upside-down roasting pan. Cook for 25–30 minutes, until soft.

Once the peppers are cooked, grill the cheese for 2–4 minutes per side, until charred.

Arrange the peppers and cheese on a platter, then scatter the marinated artichokes over the top. Serve hot or at room temperature.

GRAPEFRUIT & FENNEL PANZANELLA
WITH HONEY & WATERCRESS

Barbecued fennel is an eye-opening food revelation. The fennel softens, sweetens, intensifies, and crisps up—hands down my favorite thing to barbecue. Chop the bottom off, quarter the bulb, and you have a set of natural "cups" that char into crisps—perfect by themselves, scattered with salt. Or you can add them to this grapefruit panzanella.

Serves: 4
Prep: 15 minutes
Cook: 20 minutes

4 mini or 1 large focaccia
1 large, round fennel bulb
1 tablespoon olive oil,
   plus more for brushing
1 teaspoon sea salt flakes
2 pink or ruby grapefruit,
   quartered, skin on
1 bunch watercress

FOR THE DRESSING
1 lemon, juice only
2 tablespoons honey
2 tablespoons extra virgin olive oil
1 teaspoon sea salt flakes

Preheat the oven to 400°F (200°C). Tear or cut the focaccia into 1-inch (2½ cm) chunks and pop them onto a lined baking sheet. Bake for 20–25 minutes, until golden brown and crisp.

Prepare the fennel as described in the introduction, then put the fennel cups in a large bowl with the olive oil and sea salt flakes. Mix to coat them evenly in the oil, adding more if you wish.

Once your barbecue is good and hot, barbecue the fennel cups in batches for 3–4 minutes on each side, until crisp and charred.

Brush the grapefruit wedges with a little olive oil, then barbecue for 3–4 minutes on each side, until just charred.

Whisk the lemon juice, honey, extra virgin olive oil, and sea salt flakes together, then taste and adjust as needed.

Pile the watercress, fennel, grapefruit, and toasted focaccia on a platter, then drizzle with the dressing, mixing lightly with your hands so everything is evenly coated. Serve hot or at room temperature.

CHARRED BROCCOLINI WITH ORANGES, BLUE CHEESE & WALNUTS

This is a simple, filling side dish: broccoli and blue cheese are one of my favorite flavor combinations, and they work beautifully here with a touch of sweetness from the oranges and honey-lemon dressing.

Serves: 4
Prep: 10 minutes
Cook: 15 minutes

14 ounces (400 g) broccolini,
   blanched
Olive oil, for brushing
3 blood oranges or ordinary
   oranges, peeled and sliced
7 ounces (200 g) blue cheese,
   crumbled
A handful of toasted walnuts,
   roughly chopped

FOR THE DRESSING
2 tablespoons extra virgin olive oil
½ lemon, juice only
1 tablespoon honey
½ teaspoon sea salt flakes

Once your barbecue is good and hot, brush the broccoli spears with the olive oil and cook over high heat for 4–5 minutes, until lightly charred. Turn them over and repeat with the other side.

Whisk the extra virgin olive oil, lemon juice, honey, and sea salt flakes together for the dressing. Taste and adjust the lemon and salt as needed.

Once the broccolini is cooked, arrange on a platter with the orange slices. Drizzle with the honey dressing, top with the blue cheese and walnuts, and serve hot.

GRILLED ZUCCHINI WITH PARMESAN, ALMONDS & LEMON

This is a dish my sister used to make when we lived together, albeit she made it indoors in a griddle pan. It adapts perfectly to the barbecue—zucchini really benefits from a good char, and the combination of Parmesan, almonds, and lemon works beautifully. If you have some in the pantry, finish this off with a drop or two of good truffle oil.

Serves: 2–4 as a side
Prep: 10 minutes
Cook: 10 minutes

3 medium zucchini, cut lengthwise
    into ⅕-inch (½ cm) slices
Olive oil, for brushing
1¾ ounces (50 g) vegetarian
    Parmesan
1¾ ounces (50 g) toasted flaked
    almonds

FOR THE DRESSING
½ lemon, juice only
1 tablespoon extra virgin olive oil
1 teaspoon sea salt flakes
1 teaspoon freshly ground
    black pepper
A few drops of good truffle oil
    (optional)

Once your barbecue is good and hot, brush the zucchini slices with a little olive oil, then grill for 3–4 minutes on each side, until just charred and cooked through.

Meanwhile, whisk together the lemon juice, extra virgin olive oil, sea salt flakes, and pepper in a large bowl. Taste and adjust the salt and lemon juice as needed, and add a few drops of truffle oil, if using.

Use a peeler to shave long thin slices of Parmesan. Once the zucchini slices are cooked, gently put them in the bowl with the dressing and carefully turn them around until evenly coated.

Arrange the zucchini on a serving platter, top with the Parmesan and almonds, and serve hot.

GRILLED PAPAYA WITH TAMARIND, CHILI & COCONUT

I've been known to serve this as part of a lazy brunch outside—the papaya only gains in flavor from a short stint on the barbecue and works so well with a sharp tamarind dressing and a good sprinkle of coconut.

Serves: 4
Prep: 15 minutes
Cook: 15 minutes

1 ounce (30 g) unsweetened
  shredded coconut
⅓ ounce (10 g) fresh mint leaves,
  finely chopped
1 fresh red chili, finely chopped
1 ounce (30 g) tamarind paste,
  from a jar (not tamarind
  concentrate)
1 tablespoon olive or
  neutral oil
2 just underripe papayas, halved,
  seeds removed

Start by soaking the shredded coconut in warm water for 15 minutes, then drain well. Mix with the chopped mint leaves and red chili and set aside.

Meanwhile, mix the tamarind paste and oil together, then brush a little over the cut side of each papaya half.

Once your barbecue is good and hot, cook the papaya cut side up for 5 minutes, then flip and cook on the other side for 4–5 minutes, until it caramelizes.

Serve the grilled papaya slices hot with the remaining tamarind sauce and the coconut-chili dip alongside.

SUNSHINE SALAD: GRILLED GRAPEFRUIT & AVOCADO WITH ARUGULA & POMEGRANATE

Can you get more retro than grilled grapefruit and avocado? (Turn to page 30 to vote for cheese and pineapple on a stick or, alternatively, continue below.) Admittedly, the two feel pretty modern here: scattered with pomegranate and served with a sharp mixed citrus dressing. A refreshing dish to serve on a hot day.

Serves: 4 as a side
Prep: 15 minutes
Cook: under 15 minutes

2 avocados, not too ripe
2 tablespoons olive oil
2 pink/ruby grapefruit, halved
One 3½- to 5-ounce (100–150 g)
    bag arugula
½ pomegranate, seeds only

FOR THE DRESSING
2 tablespoons extra virgin olive oil
½ orange, zest and juice
½ lime, zest and juice
1 tablespoon agave syrup
1 teaspoon sea salt flakes

Just before you are ready to barbecue, halve and remove the stone from the avocados. Brush the avocado and grapefruit halves with the olive oil.

Barbecue the avocado and grapefruit halves for 4–5 minutes on the cut sides, brushing with more oil if needed.

To make the dressing, whisk the extra virgin olive oil, orange and lime zest and juice, agave syrup, and sea salt flakes together and set aside.

Once the avocado and grapefruit are lightly charred, remove from the barbecue and arrange with the arugula on a serving platter. Drizzle with the dressing, top with the pomegranate seeds, and serve hot.

SRI LANKAN-STYLE EGGPLANT SKEWERS & PICKLED RED ONION

After trying this Sri Lankan marinade for eggplant, I rarely want to eat it any other way—a perfect balance of chili, vinegar, and garlic along with other spices. The smoky charred eggplant works beautifully with them—and, of course, you can make this in the oven if the weather turns.

Serves: 4
Prep: 15 minutes
Cook: up to 15 minutes

3 eggplants, cut into 1-inch
   (2½ cm) cubes
1 teaspoon ground turmeric
1 teaspoon sea salt flakes
Skewers, soaked if wooden
Olive or neutral oil, for brushing

FOR THE ONIONS
½ cup (100 ml) cider or white wine
   vinegar
1 tablespoon mustard seeds
1 fresh red chili, finely chopped
1 garlic clove, finely chopped
1 teaspoon granulated sugar
1 red onion, very thinly sliced
Sea salt flakes, to taste

Mix the eggplant cubes with the turmeric and sea salt flakes in a large bowl, then thread them onto the skewers.

Once your barbecue is good and hot, brush the eggplant all over with the oil, then grill for 6–7 minutes per side, until charred and cooked through.

Meanwhile, add the cider or white wine vinegar, mustard seeds, red chili, garlic, and sugar to a pan, and bring to a boil. Add the onion and a good pinch of sea salt flakes, stir well, then lower the heat, cover, and cook for 15 minutes. The onions will soften and turn bright pink. Once cooked, taste and adjust the salt as needed.

Once the eggplant skewers are ready, pile them on a platter and dress with the pickled onions, reserving some if you wish to serve alongside. Serve hot.

Cook indoors: Pop the skewers into the oven for 30 minutes at 400°F (200°C), until the eggplant is well browned and cooked through.

BLACKENED PEPPERS WITH WALNUTS, CHILI & FENNEL SEEDS

There's a lovely Middle Eastern dip called muhamarra—roasted red peppers, walnuts, and garlic blitzed together. This dish is a sort of deconstructed version of it, with the hot charred peppers torn into large pieces and a moreish walnut, fennel, and chili pesto stirred through—a wonderful, filling side salad.

Serves: 4 as a side
Prep: 10 minutes
Cook: 20 minutes tops

3 whole mixed peppers
  (e.g. red, yellow, orange)

FOR THE WALNUT PESTO
1¾ ounces (50 g) walnuts
1 teaspoon fennel seeds
½ garlic clove
1 ounce (30 g) fresh flat-leaf parsley
¼ cup (65 ml) olive oil
½ teaspoon red pepper flakes
1 teaspoon sea salt flakes
A squeeze of lemon juice, to taste

Once your barbecue is good and hot, place the whole peppers on the grill and char them on each side until blackened.

You can make the walnut pesto in a food processor: blitz everything (except the lemon juice) together roughly, then taste and adjust with the lemon juice and salt (bearing in mind that the peppers have no salt, so a little more is fine).

Alternatively, if you don't have a food processor or feel like doing it by hand: finely chop the walnuts, fennel seeds, garlic, and parsley together on a chopping board, then stir them into the olive oil with the red pepper flakes and sea salt and adjust the seasoning as above.

Once the peppers are soft and blackened all over, remove them to your serving platter. When they're just cool enough to handle, use a spoon to scoop the stem and seeds out, then tear them into large pieces. You can also leave them whole as in the photograph opposite.

Stir most of the walnut pesto through the peppers, and scatter the rest over the top. Taste and add salt as needed, then serve hot or at room temperature.

THYME-ROASTED CHERRY TOMATOES WITH CORIANDER SEEDS & MOZZARELLA

Think of this as a sort of hot caprese salad—by cooking the tomatoes in a foil packet on the barbecue with their vines, aromatic herbs, oil, and salt, the flavors concentrate and intensify. They work beautifully with the mozzarella, as you would expect, with added interest from the crushed coriander seeds—simple yet luxurious.

Serves: 4
Prep: 10 minutes
Cook: 30 minutes

10½ ounces (300 g) cherry
   tomatoes on the vine
1 tablespoon olive oil
A few sprigs of fresh herbs
   of your choice choice: thyme,
   oregano, rosemary, or basil
1½ teaspoons sea salt flakes
1 ball of mozzarella,
   at room temperature
1 tablespoon coriander seeds,
   lightly crushed
Freshly ground black pepper
1 tablespoon extra virgin olive oil
A handful of fresh basil leaves,
   to serve

Take a large piece of foil and place the cherry tomatoes on the vine, olive oil, herbs, and 1 teaspoon of sea salt flakes in the center. Wrap it up like a parcel with the seam at the top, then place the foil packet directly on the coals for 30 minutes or on the grill if you are using a gas barbecue.

Once the tomatoes are cooked, place them onto a serving platter along with all their juices. Discard the vines, then lay the mozzarella in the middle of the dish. Top the mozzarella with the crushed coriander seeds, ½ teaspoon of sea salt flakes, and some freshly ground black pepper, and drizzle with the extra virgin olive oil.

Roughly tear the basil leaves, scatter them over everything, and serve hot or at room temperature.

Cook indoors: Put the foil packet into the oven for 30 minutes at 400°F (200°C), until the tomatoes are softened and cooked through.

SOMETHING
SUBSTANTIAL

HEARTY HERO VEGETABLES, ROBUST
ENOUGH TO TAKE CENTER STAGE.

CARB IT UP

Big veggies, big flavors. Potatoes, sweet potatoes, and squash (an honorary carb in my book).

RICOTTA WITH GRILLED SQUASH, CHARD, HONEY & HAZELNUTS   76

GUNPOWDER POTATOES WITH FENNEL SEEDS, CHILI, CILANTRO & CASHEWS (VEGAN)   78

SWEET POTATOES WITH ROSEMARY, LEMON & BLACK BEANS   80

SIMPLY BARBECUED NEW POTATOES WITH TARRAGON, PEANUTS & CHIPOTLE (VEGAN)   82

SQUASH WITH CHARRED CARROTS, RED ONIONS, CORIANDER SEEDS, PISTACHIOS & LIME (VEGAN)   84

CHERMOULA-DRESSED SWEET POTATOES & SHALLOTS WITH POMEGRANATES & MINT (VEGAN)   86

SESAME CHARRED SQUASH WITH BROCCOLINI, SPRING ONIONS, ORANGE & GINGER (VEGAN)   88

MOROCCAN GRILLED POTATOES WITH OLIVES, CHICKPEAS & PRESERVED LEMON (VEGAN)   90

RICOTTA WITH GRILLED SQUASH, CHARD, HONEY & HAZELNUTS

This is a really elegant sharing platter: let everyone help themselves to a scoop of ricotta along with the crisp, caramelized squash and charred chard (as it were). If you're having trouble finding chard, you can substitute asparagus if it's in season or broccolini.

Serves: 4
Prep: 15 minutes
Cook: 50 minutes

1.3 pounds (600 g) squash, cut into
  1-inch (2½ cm) slices
  (no need to peel)
7 ounces (200 g) Swiss or
  rainbow chard
2 teaspoons olive oil
1 teaspoon coriander seeds,
  crushed
2 teaspoons smoked paprika
1 teaspoon sea salt flakes

FOR THE DRESSING
2 tablespoons extra virgin olive oil
1 tablespoon honey
½ lemon, juice only
A pinch of sea salt flakes

TO SERVE
9 ounces (250 g) ricotta
1¾ ounces (50 g) toasted hazelnuts

Put the squash and chard in a large bowl and mix with the oil, spices, and sea salt flakes.

In a separate bowl, mix the extra virgin olive oil, honey, lemon juice, and sea salt flakes to make the dressing. Taste and adjust the salt as needed and set aside.

Once your barbecue is good and hot, lay the chard on the grill and cook for 3–5 minutes per side, until charred and cooked through. Transfer to a platter.

Lower your barbecue heat to medium, lay on the squash slices, and cook for 25 minutes on each side, covered with a roasting pan or the lid.

Once the squash is cooked through, arrange on a platter with the chard, leaving space for the ricotta in the center. Invert the ricotta, top with the hazelnuts, drizzle with the dressing, and serve hot.

GUNPOWDER POTATOES WITH FENNEL SEEDS, CHILI, CILANTRO & CASHEWS

This might be one of my favorite dishes—beautifully spiced potatoes with crisp cashews, sharp with lemon. Consider doubling the quantities if you're inviting potato fiends over, or, like the family in *The Tiger Who Came to Tea*, you'll have none left. This is also wonderful with a tablespoon of butter added just before serving and a handful of grated Cheddar (for non-vegans).

Serves: 4 as a side
Prep: 15 minutes
Cook: 1 hour

1.3 pounds (600 g) small potatoes (e.g. Yukon Gold), halved
5 tablespoons olive or neutral oil
2 garlic cloves, grated
One 1-inch (2½ cm) piece fresh ginger, grated
½ teaspoon fennel seeds, crushed
1 teaspoon coriander seeds, crushed
1 teaspoon black peppercorns, crushed
1 teaspoon cumin seeds, crushed
½ teaspoon chili powder
1½ teaspoons sea salt flakes
1 red onion, thickly sliced
1 teaspoon ground cumin
1 teaspoon ground coriander
1 lemon, juice only
1 fresh red chili, thinly sliced
A big handful of fresh cilantro leaves
1¾ ounces (50 g) toasted cashews

Put the halved potatoes in a large bowl with 3 tablespoons of the olive or neutral oil , the garlic, ginger, crushed spices (you can do these with a mortar and pestle or spice grinder), chili powder, and a teaspoon of sea salt flakes. Mix well.

In a separate bowl, mix the onion, ground cumin, ground coriander, the remaining 2 tablespoons of oil, the juice of ½ the lemon, and another ½ teaspoon of sea salt flakes. Pile the mixture in the middle of a large piece of foil and make a neat parcel with the seam on top. Set aside.

Once your barbecue is ready, lay the potatoes on the grill, cut side down, and cook covered for 20–30 minutes. Turn them over, lay the foil packet on the grill, and cook both for a further 20–30 minutes, until the potatoes are cooked through and the onions are tender.

Mix the onions and potatoes in a serving dish, adding the spiced oil from the foil packet, and mix in the chili, the rest of the lemon juice, and the cilantro leaves. Taste and adjust the salt as needed, then top with the cashews and serve hot.

SWEET POTATOES
WITH ROSEMARY, LEMON & BLACK BEANS

Baking sweet potatoes whole in their skins intensifies and sweetens the flesh—one of my favorite ways to cook them. And, if you cook them directly on the coals, there's a wonderful smokiness upon serving. I like to do this once I've finished barbecuing other bits and pieces, when there's still a good amount of heat left in the barbecue.

Serves: 6 as a side
Prep: 10 minutes
Cook: 45 minutes–1 hour

6 small sweet potatoes, whole
One 15-ounce (425 g) can of
   black beans, drained and rinsed
1 lemon, juice only
3 tablespoons olive oil
2 sprigs fresh rosemary leaves,
   finely chopped
¾ ounce (20 g) fresh flat-leaf
   parsley, roughly chopped
6 tablespoons Greek yogurt

Place the sweet potatoes directly on the coals, or on the grill if cooking on gas, and let them cook for 45 minutes to an hour, turning halfway, until completely soft all the way through.

Meanwhile, mix the black beans, lemon juice, olive oil, rosemary, and flat-leaf parsley in a bowl. Cover and leave to marinate.

Once the sweet potatoes are cooked through, dust off any coal, split them down the middle, and stuff with the black bean mixture and a spoonful of Greek yogurt in each. Serve hot.

Cook indoors: Lightly oil the sweet potatoes and roast whole in the oven on a lined baking sheet for 45 minutes to 1 hour at 400°F (200°C).

SIMPLY BARBECUED NEW POTATOES
WITH TARRAGON, PEANUTS & CHIPOTLE

The dressing for this dish is unusual—smoky chili peanuts combined with tarragon—and somewhat addictive, especially when paired with crisp barbecued potatoes. You could easily use this as a dressing for grilled corn or mushrooms.

Serves: 4
Prep: 15 minutes
Cook: 30 minutes

1.3 pounds (600 g) new potatoes
2 tablespoons olive oil
1 teaspoon sea salt flakes

FOR THE DRESSING
⅓ ounce (10 g) fresh tarragon
  leaves, finely chopped
1 ounce (30 g) unsalted peanuts,
  finely chopped
3 tablespoons extra virgin olive oil
2 tablespoons lemon juice
A pinch of red pepper flakes
A pinch of sea salt flakes

Boil the potatoes in salted water for 7–8 minutes, until just cooked through. Drain well, then mix with the olive oil and sea salt flakes.

Mix together the tarragon, peanuts, extra virgin olive oil, lemon juice, red pepper flakes, and sea salt flakes to make the dressing. Taste and adjust the salt as needed, then set aside.

Once your barbecue is good and hot, grill the potatoes for 5–8 minutes per side, until nicely charred.

Halve the barbecued new potatoes, mix with the tarragon dressing, and serve hot.

Note: If you have time, you can leave out the boiling stage and just cook the potatoes on the barbecue, in which case they will take about 1 hour.

SQUASH WITH CHARRED CARROTS, RED ONIONS, CORIANDER SEEDS, PISTACHIOS & LIME

A substantial and moreish main dish. The natural sugars in squash and carrots caramelize beautifully on the barbecue and work perfectly with the aromatic lime and spices.

Serves: 4
Prep: 15 minutes
Cook: 50 minutes

1.3 pounds (600 g) squash, cut into
   1-inch (2½ cm) slices
   (no need to peel)
5 ounces (150 g) baby carrots,
   whole and unpeeled (or 3 medium
   carrots, peeled and halved)
1 red onion, quartered, core intact
2 teaspoons olive oil
1 teaspoon coriander seeds,
   crushed
1 teaspoon ground cumin
1 teaspoon sea salt flakes
1¾ ounces (50 g) pistachios,
   roughly chopped

FOR THE DRESSING
2 tablespoons extra virgin olive oil
1 lime, zest and juice
2 teaspoons coriander seeds,
   crushed
½ teaspoon black peppercorns,
   crushed
1 teaspoon sea salt flakes

Put the squash, carrots, and red onion in a large bowl and mix with the oil, spices, and sea salt flakes.

In a separate bowl, mix the extra virgin olive oil, lime zest and juice, coriander seeds, crushed black pepper, and sea salt flakes. Taste and adjust the salt as needed and set aside.

Once your barbecue is ready, lay the squash slices on the grill and cook for 25 minutes on each side, covered if you can. The carrots and the onions should only take about 15 minutes per side, so put them on 10 minutes after the squash and take them off 10 minutes before the squash.

Once the vegetables are all cooked through, transfer them to a platter and gently mix with the lime and coriander seed dressing. Top with the pistachios and serve hot or warm.

CHERMOULA-DRESSED SWEET POTATOES & SHALLOTS WITH POMEGRANATES & MINT

Think about a good, fresh pesto, then think about it made with fresh cilantro, mint, preserved lemon, and warming spices. Voila! You have chermoula, a North African herb-and-spice mix. It's wonderful as an accompaniment or dip for pretty much everything that comes off a barbecue, and particularly with charred sweet potatoes and shallots, as in this recipe.

Serves: 4
Prep: 15 minutes
Cook: 50 minutes

4 small sweet potatoes, halved
8 echalion shallots, whole, unpeeled
2 tablespoons olive oil
A pinch of sea salt flakes

FOR THE CHERMOULA
½ ounce (15 g) fresh cilantro,
   leaves and stems
½ ounce (15 g) mint, leaves only
1 heaped teaspoon ground cumin
1 heaped teaspoon ground paprika
3 garlic cloves, peeled
2 tablespoons olive oil
A pinch of sea salt flakes
1 preserved lemon,
   or zest of ½ lemon,
   plus 1 teaspoon white vinegar
½ pomegranate, seeds only,
   to serve

Mix the halved sweet potatoes and whole shallots with the oil and sea salt flakes in a large bowl until evenly coated.

Once your barbecue is medium hot, arrange the potatoes and onions on the grill and cover with an upside-down roasting pan or the lid. Cook for 25 minutes, then turn them over and cook for a further 25 minutes or until the sweet potatoes are cooked through and the onions are soft.

Meanwhile, blitz together all the ingredients for the chermoula (or finely chop them by hand). Taste and adjust the salt and lemon as needed.

Once the sweet potatoes and onions are cooked, carefully halve the onions and slip them out of their skins. Arrange the vegetables on a platter, drizzle with the chermoula, top with the pomegranate seeds, and serve hot.

SESAME CHARRED SQUASH WITH BROCCOLINI, SPRING ONIONS, ORANGE & GINGER

I love the Asian flavors in this dish: the sweetness of the squash works beautifully with the sesame, orange, and ginger.

Serves: 4
Prep: 15 minutes
Cook: 50 minutes

1.3 pounds (600 g) squash, cut into 1-inch (2½ cm) slices
7 ounces (200 g) broccolini, blanched
2 tablespoons sesame oil
2 garlic cloves, grated
1 teaspoon sea salt flakes
½ teaspoon red pepper flakes
½ teaspoon Szechuan peppercorns, crushed

FOR THE DRESSING
2 tablespoons sesame oil
½ orange, zest and juice
One 1-inch (2½ cm) piece fresh ginger, grated
1 tablespoon sesame seeds
½ teaspoon sea salt flakes
3 spring onions, thinly sliced

Put the squash and broccolini in a large bowl and mix with the oil, garlic, sea salt flakes, red pepper flakes, and Szechuan peppercorns.

In a separate bowl, mix the sesame oil, orange zest and juice, ginger, sesame seeds, sea salt flakes, and spring onions. Taste and adjust the salt as needed, then set aside.

Once your barbecue is good and hot, lay the broccolini on the grill and cook for 3–5 minutes per side, until just charred and cooked through. Transfer to a platter.

Once your barbecue is medium hot, lay the squash slices on the grill and cook for 25 minutes per side, covered with a roasting pan or the lid.

Once the squash is cooked through, arrange on the platter with the broccolini. Drizzle with the sesame dressing and serve hot.

MOROCCAN GRILLED POTATOES WITH OLIVES, CHICKPEAS & PRESERVED LEMON

This dish is inspired by one of my favorite tagines, which we made in a field kitchen in the desert on location for a film shoot in the Sahara. Olives, preserved lemon, and potatoes work beautifully together; along with the chickpeas, this is almost a meal in itself. Forgive the lack of chickpeas in the photograph—I forgot to buy them and couldn't bring myself to open the fancy jarred kind at my publisher's house.

Serves: 4
Prep: 15 minutes
Cook: 30 minutes

1.3 pounds (600 g) new potatoes
2 tablespoons olive oil
1 teaspoon ground coriander
1 teaspoon ground cumin
½ teaspoon ground turmeric
1 teaspoon sea salt flakes
A handful of fresh mint, to serve

FOR THE CHICKPEAS
One 15-ounce (425 g) can
    chickpeas, drained and rinsed
1 red onion, finely chopped
2¾ ounces (80 g) pitted green
    olives
1 preserved lemon, finely chopped
2 tablespoons olive oil

Boil the new potatoes in salted water for 7–8 minutes, until just cooked through. Drain well, then mix with the olive oil, ground coriander, cumin, turmeric, and sea salt flakes.

Take a large piece of foil and add the chickpeas, onion, olives, preserved lemon, and olive oil. Fold into a neat packet with the seam at the top.

While your barbecue is heating up, place the foil packet directly on the coals, or on the grill if using gas. Once your barbecue is good and hot, grill the potatoes for 5–8 minutes per side, until nicely charred.

When the potatoes are cooked through, halve them and place on a serving platter. Open the foil packet of chickpeas and gently add them to the potatoes. Taste and adjust the salt as needed, top with the fresh mint, and serve hot.

DAIRY-ISH

Feta, paneer, and tofu—the paneer and tofu recipes are helpfully interchangeable, so you can veganize as you wish.

SRIRACHA-GRILLED TOFU WITH PICKLED ONIONS, LIME & CILANTRO (VEGAN) 94

PANEER WITH HARISSA, GREEN BEANS, CHICKPEAS & LIME 96

CRISPY BARBECUE TOFU LETTUCE WRAPS WITH CASHEWS, CARROTS & NUOC CHAM (VEGAN) 98

VIETNAMESE GRILLED TOFU WITH TOMATOES & SPRING ONIONS (VEGAN) 100

CHARRED PANEER & FENNEL WITH CHILI ALMONDS, LEMON & DILL 102

DILL-DRENCHED FETA WITH BEETS, CUCUMBER, APPLE & WATERCRESS 104

SPICED PANEER WITH MANGO, AVOCADO, CHILI & CILANTRO 106

GRILLED FETA, PINEAPPLE & BLACK BEAN TACOS WITH CHILI & LIME 108

SRIRACHA-GRILLED TOFU
WITH PICKLED ONIONS, LIME & CILANTRO

This is such a quick dish to throw together. Watch out for the sriracha, as it varies in strength by brand—the tablespoon used below was fiery, so by all means adapt it to your taste.

Serves: 4
Prep: 10 minutes
Cook: 15 minutes tops

One 10-ounce (280 g) block firm tofu
1 tablespoon sriracha
1 tablespoon olive or netural oil
1 teaspoon sea salt flakes
A large handful of fresh cilantro, chopped

FOR THE DRESSING
½ red onion, thinly sliced
1 lime, zest and juice
A pinch of sea salt flakes

Cut the tofu into four pieces lengthwise and place them in a bowl with the sriracha, oil, and sea salt flakes. Turn gently to coat and set aside.

Blanch the red onion in a small pan of boling water for 30 seconds before draining well. Mix with the lime zest and juice and a pinch of sea salt, then set aside.

Once your barbecue is good and hot, grill the tofu for 3–4 minutes on each side, until well charred. Serve with the pickled onions, cilantro, and a scattering of sea salt flakes.

PANEER WITH HARISSA, GREEN BEANS, CHICKPEAS & LIME

Store–bought paneer works perfectly on the barbecue—crisp and charred on the outside and, if you time it right, soft on the inside. This version, spiced with harissa and served with crunchy green beans and marinated chickpeas, is perfect with flatbread served alongside.

Serves: 4
Prep: 15 minutes
Cook: 20 minutes

One 15-ounce (425 g) can
  chickpeas, drained and rinsed
¾ ounce (20 g) fresh cilantro,
  roughly chopped
1 lime, juice only
2 teaspoons sea salt flakes
3 tablespoons olive oil
8 ounces (225 g) paneer, cut into
  1-inch (2½ cm) cubes
5 ounces (150 g) green beans
1 heaped tablespoon harissa
Yogurt and flatbreads, to serve

Mix the chickpeas with the cilantro, lime juice, 1 teaspoon of sea salt flakes, and 1 tablespoon of olive oil. Taste and adjust the seasoning as needed, then cover and set aside.

Put the paneer and green beans in a large bowl with the harissa, the remaining teaspoon of sea salt flakes, and the remaining 2 tablespoons of olive oil, and mix well. Set aside until you're ready to barbecue.

Once your barbecue is good and hot, grill the green beans for a few minutes on each side until charred and cooked through, then set them aside. Repeat with the paneer until crisp and charred—don't let it cook for too long, or you'll lose the softness of the inside.

Put the paneer back into the bowl with the leftover marinade and gently stir it through to coat.

Pile the green beans, paneer, and marinated chickpeas on a platter, and serve with yogurt and flatbreads.

CRISPY BARBECUE TOFU LETTUCE WRAPS WITH CASHEWS, CARROTS & NUOC CHAM

This is a combination I first tried in Vietnam—nuoc cham is such an addictive dipping sauce that it's tempting to drink it straight up. If you can resist, save some and use it for your crispy tofu instead.

Serves: 4
Prep: 15 minutes
Cook: 10 minutes

FOR THE TOFU
10 ounces (280 g) firm tofu
1 lime, zest and juice
1 tablespoon soy sauce
1 garlic clove, grated
1 tablespoon sesame oil
Pinch of sea salt flakes

FOR THE CARROT PICKLE
1 medium carrot,
   cut into matchsticks
1 tablespoon rice vinegar
1 teaspoon granulated sugar
½ teaspoon sea salt flakes

FOR THE NUOC CHAM
1 garlic clove
1 fresh red chili, roughly chopped
One 1-inch (2½ cm) piece fresh
   ginger
1–2 tablespoons soy sauce
¼ cup (50 ml) water
½ lime, zest and juice

TO SERVE
1 small head romaine lettuce, leaves
   separated
A handful of toasted cashews

Cut the tofu into large cubes and put them into a bowl with the lime zest and juice, soy sauce, garlic, and sesame oil. Mix gently to coat, then cover and set aside.

For the carrot pickle, mix the carrot matchsticks with the rice vinegar, sugar, and sea salt flakes. Cover and set aside.

To make the nuoc cham, put the garlic, chili, and ginger in a mortar and crush into a paste with a pestle. (Alternatively, grate all the ingredients into a jar.) Add the soy sauce, water, lime zest and juice, and taste. Adjust the amount of soy, water, and lime as needed and set aside.

When your barbecue is good and hot, grill the marinated tofu for 2–3 minutes per side, until lightly charred and crisp. Scatter with a pinch of sea salt.

Arrange the lettuce leaves on a platter and add a spoonful of carrot pickle to each. Divide the crispy tofu among the lettuce leaves, scatter with the toasted cashews and a drizzle of nuoc cham, and serve the remaining nuoc cham alongside.

VIETNAMESE GRILLED TOFU
WITH TOMATOES & SPRING ONIONS

This is one dish that I didn't manage to try while in Vietnam but ate instead at a very good Vietnamese restaurant in Chicago. It's a simple dish, packed with intense flavor from the tomatoes. In this version, I barbecue the tofu for extra flavor and texture.

Serves: 4
Prep: 15 minutes
Cook: 50 minutes

9 ounces (250 g) cherry tomatoes
   on the vine
1 tablespoon tomato paste
2 teaspoons sea salt flakes
1 teaspoon sugar
1 garlic clove, unpeeled
10 ounces (280 g) firm tofu
2 tablespoons sesame or neutral oil
1 teaspoon freshly ground black
   pepper

TO SERVE
4 spring onions, thinly sliced
1 lime, zest and juice

Take a large piece of foil and place the cherry tomatoes, their vines, the tomato paste, 1 teaspoon of the sea salt flakes, sugar, and garlic in the middle. Fold it up to make a neat packet with the seam on the top.

Press the liquid out of the tofu, using your hands and a clean tea towel or paper towel, then cut it into ½-inch- (1½ cm) deep triangles. Gently dress them in a bowl with the oil, the remaining teaspoon of the sea salt flakes, and pepper.

Once your barbecue is good and hot, place the tomato packet directly on the coals, or on the grill if cooking with gas, and set a timer for 15 minutes. Barbecue the tofu for 4–5 minutes per side, until crisp and golden brown.

Once the tomatoes are cooked, put them in a bowl and squash them with a wooden spoon. Gently add the crispy tofu, top with the spring onions and lime zest and juice, and serve hot or at room temperature. (What you lose in crispness by letting the dish sit, you gain in flavor.)

CHARRED PANEER & FENNEL
WITH CHILI ALMONDS, LEMON & DILL

In this dish, the lightly spiced paneer combines with crisp almonds and sweet, caramelized fennel—a lovely, elegant sharing plate.

Serves: 4
Prep: 20 minutes
Cook: 15 minutes

1¾ ounces (50 g) blanched almonds
1 teaspoon butter
½ teaspoon red pepper flakes
A pinch of sea salt flakes
One 8-ounce (225 g) block paneer
1 round fennel bulb
1 tablespoon olive oil

FOR THE SPICE PASTE
1 teaspoon fennel seeds
1 teaspoon coriander seeds
1 tablespoon olive oil
1 tablespoon sea salt flakes
1 tablespoon tomato paste

FOR THE DRESSING
½ lemon, juice and zest
½ ounce (15 g) fresh dill, roughly
  chopped
2 tablespoons oil
A pinch of sea salt
Freshly ground black pepper

Start by mixing the blanched almonds, butter, red pepper flakes, and sea salt flakes on a small lined baking sheet and toast for 10 minutes at 325°F (160°C), until just golden brown. While the almonds are in the oven, cut the paneer into four rectangles.

Roughly crush the fennel and coriander seeds with a mortar and pestle, then mix with the oil, sea salt flakes, and tomato paste. Rub the spice paste all over the paneer and leave to marinate for at least 10 minutes.

Meanwhile, cut the stem off the fennel, quarter it, then pull apart so you have a series of small cups. Mix them in a bowl with the olive oil.

For the dressing, mix together the lemon juice and zest, dill, oil, salt, and black pepper. Taste and adjust the seasoning as needed.

When your barbecue is good and hot, grill the paneer and fennel cups on both sides in batches, turning them over halfway through. You want the paneer just charred but still soft on the inside, and the fennel cups cooked through and charring around the edges—about 2–3 minutes per side for the paneer if the barbecue is very hot and 3–4 minutes per side for the fennel.

Pile the charred fennel and paneer onto a serving platter, drizzle with the dressing, scatter with the chili almonds, and serve hot.

DILL-DRENCHED FETA WITH BEETS, CUCUMBER, APPLE & WATERCRESS

If you're using a charcoal barbecue, this dish is perfect to make toward the end—place the beet cubes into a foil packet with lemon, lay them directly on the coals, and let them cook. Of course, you could also pop your foil packet into the oven and have this as an accompanying salad to your barbecue—I find the combination of sweet apple, beets, cucumber, and feta mildly addictive.

Serves: 4
Prep: 15 minutes
Cook: 1 hour

1.8 pounds (800 g) beets, peeled and cut into ½-inch (1½ cm) chunks
A pinch of sea salt flakes
Freshly ground black pepper
1 tablespoon olive oil
½ lemon, juice only
1 apple, cut into ½-inch (1½ cm) chunks
5 ounces (150 g) cucumber, cut into ½-inch (1½ cm) chunks
1 bunch of watercress
1 block of good feta cheese
1 ounce (30 g) fresh dill, chopped

FOR THE DRESSING
2 tablespoons extra virgin olive oil
½ lemon, juice only
A pinch of sea salt flakes
Freshly ground black pepper

Cook indoors: Put the foil packet of beets on a baking tray and cook in the oven for 1 hour at 425°F (220°C).

Put the beets, sea salt flakes, black pepper, olive oil, and lemon juice—and the squeezed-out lemon half, if you like—in the middle of a large piece of foil, then carefully wrap it into a packet with the seam at the top.

Place the packet directly on the coals, or on one side of the grill if using gas, and let it cook for 45 minutes to 1 hour, until the beets are just tender.

Meanwhile, mix the olive oil, lemon juice, sea salt flakes, and freshly ground pepper together for the dressing and set aside.

Once the beets are cooked, combine with the apple and cucumber and one-third of the dressing. Scatter the watercress over your serving plate and dress with another third of the dressing. Tumble the beets, apple, and cucumber over the top.

Flash-grill the block of feta cheese on the barbecue for 2 minutes per side (watching carefully to make sure it doesn't melt through) or under a hot broiler for a few minutes, then lay it on top of the salad. Drizzle with the remaining lemon dressing, scatter with the dill, and serve.

SPICED PANEER WITH MANGO, AVOCADO, CHILI & CILANTRO

Middle Eastern dishes liberally use herbs in the way that we would use salad leaves, so if you like cilantro, this is the dish for you. The sweetness of the mango against the avocado and lightly spiced paneer makes this a substantial salad, excellent with flatbread and yogurt on the side.

Serves: 4 as a side
Prep: 20 minutes
Cook: under 15 minutes

One 8-ounce (225 g) block paneer,
    cut into triangles
2 tablespoons olive oil
1 teaspoon cayenne pepper
2 garlic cloves, grated
One 1-inch (2½ cm) piece fresh
    ginger, grated
1 teaspoon sea salt flakes
1 lime, zest and juice
1 large, just underripe mango
1 large, just underripe avocado
Massive handfuls of cilantro
    leaves

FOR THE DRESSING
2 tablespoons olive oil
1 lime, zest and juice
1 fresh red chili, finely chopped
A pinch of sea salt flakes

Note: I am far too lazy to pick cilantro leaves by hand, but as you don't want stalks in this salad, the easiest thing to do is to buy a living pot of cilantro from the supermarket and give it a haircut just below the leaves before serving.

Mix the paneer triangles with a tablespoon of olive oil, the cayenne pepper, garlic, ginger, sea salt flakes, and lime zest and juice, and set aside to marinate at room temperature for 45 minutes, or overnight in the fridge.

For the dressing, mix the olive oil, lime zest and juice, red chili, and sea salt flakes, taste and adjust the salt as needed, then set aside.

Take the cheeks off the mango and halve each so you have 4 long wedges. Just before you are ready to barbecue, halve the avocado and remove the stone, then cut the flesh into quarters. Brush the avocado and mango slices with the other tablespoon of olive oil.

Once the barbecue is ready, cook the marinated paneer, avocado, and mango slices for 4–5 minutes on each of the cut sides, brushing with more oil if needed. You'll want to take the avocado off as soon as you have a few char lines; they're at their best just warmed through. The mango benefits from a longer cook.

Once the fruit and paneer are nicely charred, transfer them to a serving platter and gently mix with the lime and chili dressing and the cilantro leaves. Taste, adjust the seasoning as needed, and serve immediately.

GRILLED FETA, PINEAPPLE & BLACK BEAN TACOS WITH CHILI & LIME

Is this dish another attempt to get cheese and pineapple out of the '80s and back into the mainstream? Potentially. But no one can fault the combination of hot grilled pineapple with chili, feta, and lime-marinated black beans. Serve with margaritas.

Serves: 4
Prep: 15 minutes
Cook: 20 minutes

1 pineapple, peeled, cored,
    and cut into eighths
1 teaspoon red pepper flakes
1 tablespoon olive oil
One 9-ounce (250 g) block feta
A handful of fresh mint leaves, torn
One 15-ounce (425 g) can black
    beans, drained and rinsed
1 tablespoon extra virgin olive oil
1 lime, zest and juice
8 tortillas, warmed

Stir the pineapple slices with the red pepper flakes and olive oil and set aside.

Wrap the feta in a piece of foil with a few of the mint leaves. Put the black beans, extra virgin olive oil, and lime zest and juice into another piece of foil and wrap it up in a neat parcel, making sure both parcels have the seam on the top.

Once your barbecue is good and hot, place the packet of black beans directly on the coals, or onto the grill if using gas. Pop the packet of feta on one side of the grill, then grill the pineapple for 4–5 minutes on each side, until just charred.

Once the pineapple is all cooked, put the black beans in a bowl, stir in the rest of the torn fresh mint, and crumble through the warm feta. Taste and adjust the lime juice as needed. Pile the pineapple onto a serving platter and serve with the warm tortillas for people to make their own tacos.

QUICK PREP, QUICK COOK

Corn, eggplant, mushrooms—simple dishes with just a handful of ingredients.

FIVE-SPICE EGGPLANT WITH BOK CHOY & LIME (VEGAN)   112

BARBECUED CORN WITH GINGER, PEANUT & CHILI DRESSING (VEGAN)   114

GRILLED PORTOBELLO MUSHROOMS & LEEKS WITH TARRAGON & WALNUTS (VEGAN)   118

BARBECUED CORN WITH SAGE & PINE NUT BUTTER   120

OREGANO, PINE NUT & MOZZARELLA–STUFFED MUSHROOMS WITH CHILI   122

GRILLED EGGPLANT WITH CUCUMBER, WALNUTS & CUMIN (VEGAN)   126

SPICED PARMESAN CORN WITH LEMON & MINT   128

YUZU MUSHROOMS WITH CILANTRO & CASHEWS (VEGAN)   130

HALLOUMI–STUFFED EGGPLANT WITH LEMON & OREGANO   132

FIVE-SPICE EGGPLANT
WITH BOK CHOY & LIME

Chinese five-spice powder gives a wonderful earthy flavor to this egg-plant—paired with crisp, charred bok choy and a light dressing, this makes an easy, flavorful platter.

Serves: 4
Prep: 15 minutes
Cook: 20 minutes

3 eggplants, cut into ½-inch (1½ cm) slices
3 teaspoons Chinese five-spice powder
1½ teaspoons sea salt flakes, plus more to taste
4 bok choy, halved
Olive or other neutral oil, for brushing
2 limes, juice only
A handful of chopped fresh chives or cilantro

Toss the eggplant pieces, five-spice, sea salt flakes, and bok choy in a large bowl.

Once your barbecue is good and hot, fish the egg-plant out of the bowl, brush liberally with oil, and barbecue for 3–5 minutes each side, until charred and cooked through.

Set the eggplant aside on a platter, then repeat with the bok choy for 2–3 minutes each side, until wilted and just cooked through.

Scatter the bok choy over the eggplant, dress with the lime juice, taste and add sea salt flakes as needed, then serve scattered with the chopped chives or cilantro.

BARBECUED CORN
WITH GINGER, PEANUT & CHILI DRESSING

One of the most popular recipes in *The Green Roasting Tin* is the Indonesian gado-gado: crunchy potatoes with an addictive peanut, coconut, and chili sauce. It occurred to me that the dressing, slightly adapted, would work beautifully with grilled corn on the cob—and joy, it did! This is now a summer staple.

Serves: 6
Prep: 10 minutes
Cook: 20 minutes

6 ears corn on the cob
2½ tablespoons olive
   or neutral oil
1 teaspoon sea salt flakes
1¾ ounces (50 g) crunchy
   peanut butter
⅓ cup (80 ml) coconut milk
2 tablespoons (30 ml) lime juice
1½ tablespoons soy sauce
One 1-inch (2½ cm) piece fresh
   ginger, finely chopped/grated
1 fresh red chili, finely chopped
⅓ ounce (10 g) fresh chives,
   finely chopped

In a large bowl, evenly coat the corn with the oil and sea salt flakes.

Mix together the peanut butter, coconut milk, lime juice, soy sauce, ginger, chili, and chives.

Once your barbecue is good and hot, cook the corn for 4–5 minutes on each side, turning as each side grills, until the whole cob is evenly charred to your liking.

Serve the grilled corn with the sauce alongside, and let people spoon the dressing on top.

Cook indoors: Roast the corn in the oven for 45 minutes at 400°F (200°C) and serve with the dressing as above.

GRILLED PORTOBELLO MUSHROOMS & LEEKS WITH TARRAGON & WALNUTS

This is a robust dish with big hits of flavor from the tarragon and walnuts. Serve with good bread.

Serves: 4
Prep: 15 minutes
Cook: 20 minutes

4 medium leeks
1.3 pounds (600 g) portobello
  mushrooms, whole
4 tablespoons olive oil
1 teaspoon sea salt flakes

FOR THE DRESSING
3 tablespoons extra virgin olive oil
1 lemon, zest and juice
⅓ ounce (10 g) fresh tarragon,
  leaves only, finely chopped
1¾ ounces (50 g) walnuts,
  roughly chopped
1 teaspoon sea salt flakes

Leave the tough outer skin on the leeks, trim off the green tops, then slice them into 2-inch (5 cm) logs. Put them in a large bowl with the mushrooms, then add the olive oil and sea salt flakes and gently mix until evenly coated.

For the dressing, stir together the olive oil, lemon zest and juice, tarragon, walnuts, and sea salt flakes. Taste and adjust the salt and lemon as needed, then set aside.

Once your barbecue is good and hot, grill the leeks and mushrooms, turning them every 5 minutes, until the mushrooms are cooked through and the leeks are charred on the outside and soft within—this should take 15–20 minutes.

Discard the outer, very charred skin from the leeks if you wish. Arrange on a platter with the mushrooms, drizzle with the tarragon and walnut dressing, and serve hot.

BARBECUED CORN
WITH SAGE & PINE NUT BUTTER

This is, if I may say so myself, an inspired way to dress crisp grilled corn. Crunch from the pine nuts, sage warmed through by the melting butter—a bit like your favorite ravioli dressing, albeit on a different carb. Use a plant-based spread or good olive oil for a vegan version of this dish.

Serves: 4
Prep: 10 minutes
Cook: 20 minutes

4 ears corn on the cob
2 tablespoons olive oil
1½ teaspoons sea salt flakes
1 tablespoon butter
1 tablespoon pine nuts, chopped
10 fresh sage leaves, finely chopped
½ garlic clove, finely chopped

In a large bowl, evenly coat the corn with the oil and 1 teaspoon of sea salt flakes.

Mix the butter, pine nuts, sage leaves, garlic, and ½ teaspoon of sea salt flakes and set aside.

Once your barbecue is good and hot, cook the corn for 4–5 minutes on each side, turning as each side grills, until the whole cob is evenly charred to your liking.

Spread the sage and pine nut butter over the corn as soon as it comes off the barbecue and serve hot.

Cook indoors: Roast the corn in the oven for 45 minutes at 400°F (200°C) and dress with the butter as above.

OREGANO, PINE NUT & MOZZARELLA-STUFFED MUSHROOMS WITH CHILI

I love a stuffed mushroom; these supersized offerings take minutes to put together and taste like a hot summer day in the Mediterranean. To veganize, use good chopped seasoned tofu or plant-based soft cheese as an alternative to the mozzarella. Serve in buns, like burgers, or with ciabatta on the side.

Serves: 4
Prep: 10 minutes
Cook: 15 minutes

9 ounces (250 g) mozzarella, roughly chopped
⅓ ounce (10 g) fresh oregano, leaves only
1 ounce (30 g) pine nuts
½ fresh red chili, finely chopped
½ lemon, zest and juice
1 teaspoon sea salt flakes
4–6 giant portobello mushrooms, stems removed
Olive oil, for brushing

TO SERVE
¾ ounce (20 g) pine nuts, roughly chopped
⅕ ounce (5 g) fresh oregano, leaves only
½ fresh red chili, finely chopped

Mix the mozzarella, oregano, pine nuts, chili, lemon zest and juice, and sea salt flakes together. Taste and adjust the salt as needed and set aside.

Once your barbecue is good and hot, brush the mushrooms all over with olive oil and place on the barbecue with the side you're going to fill down and the smooth side up. Cook for 7–10 minutes, until softened, then flip them over.

Carefully fill the mushroom caps with the mozzarella mixture, packing it down gently with a spoon. (You may wish to take the mushrooms off the barbecue and put them on a plate to do this.)

Cook the mushrooms smooth side down, filling side up, for a further 7–10 minutes—if you've got particularly giant mushrooms, you can cook them with the barbecue lid down or by putting an upside-down roasting pan or bowl over the top to create an oven effect.

Once the mushrooms are cooked through and the mozzarella has melted, arrange on a plate, scatter with the pine nuts, oregano, and chili, and serve hot.

GRILLED EGGPLANT
WITH CUCUMBER, WALNUTS & CUMIN

I love this dish, with the hot, blackened eggplant against the crisp, cold cucumber and the warming walnut and cumin—a refreshing combination and perfect for a hot day. Eggplant cooked on the barbecue tastes like nothing else, but I've given options for making this dish indoors as well so you can have it year-round.

Serves:	4 as a side
Prep:	10 minutes
Cook:	20 minutes tops

2 eggplants, cut into ⅓-inch (1 cm) slices
2 teaspoons sea salt flakes
2 teaspoons cumin seeds, roughly ground
2 tablespoons olive oil, plus more for brushing
½ cucumber, cut into ⅓-inch (1 cm) slices
2 tablespoons walnuts, roughly chopped
½ lemon, juice only

Rub the eggplant slices with half the salt and roughly ground cumin seeds. Once your barbecue is good and hot, brush the eggplant on both sides with the olive oil and place on the barbecue grill. Cook for 4–5 minutes, until well charred, then flip and repeat on the other side until cooked through.

Meanwhile, mix the cucumber, remaining sea salt and roughly ground cumin, oil, walnuts, and lemon juice together, and leave to marinate.

Once the eggplant is cooked, arrange on a platter and scatter with the cucumber and walnut mix. Serve hot or at room temperature.

Cook indoors: Cook the eggplant as above but in batches in a ridged griddle pan, or roast in a single layer on a large baking sheet for about 25 minutes at 425°F (220°C), until well browned and cooked through.

SPICED PARMESAN CORN WITH LEMON & MINT

The secret ingredient in this spiced corn is cumin—it works so well with the Parmesan. Addictive, as all barbecued corn is.

Serves: 4–6
Prep: 10 minutes
Cook: 15 minutes

4–6 ears corn on the cob
2 tablespoons olive oil
¼ teaspoon cayenne pepper
1 teaspoon ground cumin
1 teaspoon sea salt flakes
1½ ounces (40 g) vegetarian
    Parmesan, finely grated
A handful of fresh mint,
    finely chopped
Juice of 1 lemon

Combine the corn, olive oil, cayenne, cumin, and sea salt flakes in a large bowl and mix until the corn is completely coated in the spices and oil.

Once your barbecue is good and hot, cook the corn for 2–3 minutes on all sides, until evenly charred.

Meanwhile, add your grated Parmesan to a roasting pan large enough to hold all four pieces of corn on the cob. As soon as the corn is cooked and off the barbecue, place it in the pan with the cheese and give it a good shake to evenly coat the corn. The cheese will start melting into the hot corn. Then top with the chopped mint and a squeeze of lemon and serve with skewers to eat as soon as you can.

YUZU MUSHROOMS WITH CILANTRO & CASHEWS

You can find tiny bottles of yuzu juice along with Japanese rice vinegar and soy in larger supermarkets—it's the juice of a Southeast Asian citrus fruit, like a more floral and very addictive version of lime juice. The splurge is worth it for this unusual side dish—you can use it instead of lime juice in other Asian-style dressings too.

Serves: 4
Prep: 10 minutes
Cook: 15 minutes

1.3 pounds (600 g) portobello mushrooms, whole
3 tablespoons sesame oil
1 teaspoon sea salt flakes
A handful of chopped fresh cilantro
A handful of toasted cashews, chopped

FOR THE DRESSING
3 tablespoons yuzu juice
2 tablespoons sesame oil
A pinch of sea salt flakes

Toss the mushrooms in a large bowl with the sesame oil and sea salt flakes.

For the dressing, stir the yuzu juice, sesame oil, and sea salt flakes together. Taste and adjust the salt and yuzu as needed, then set aside.

Once your barbecue is good and hot, grill the mushrooms, turning them every 5 minutes until they are cooked through—this should take 15–20 minutes.

Arrange the mushrooms on a platter, drizzle with the yuzu dressing, and scatter the chopped cilantro and cashews on top. (Eagle-eyed readers may note that there are no cashews opposite: we'd eaten half the dish before realizing I'd left them in the oven. But don't let that stop you from using them!)

HALLOUMI-STUFFED EGGPLANT
WITH LEMON & OREGANO

In this dish, thinly sliced eggplant is softened on the barbecue while you marinate sticks of halloumi in lemon, oregano, and mint. When the eggplant is just soft, you roll the slices around the cheese and return them to the barbecue to char: one of my favorite recipes.

Serves: 4
Prep: 15 minutes
Cook: under 15 minutes

2 fat eggplants
Olive oil, for brushing
9 ounces (250 g) halloumi, cut into
    ½-inch (1½ cm) rectangular sticks
2 tablespoons fresh mint leaves,
    roughly chopped
2 tablespoons fresh oregano
    leaves, roughly chopped
1 lemon, juice only
Toothpicks
2 tablespoons extra virgin olive oil

Cut each eggplant into eight thin slices, then brush the slices on one side with olive oil. Once your barbecue is hot (you can pop these on as the barbecue is just getting warm, too), put the eggplant slices on, oil side down, and brush the tops with a little more oil. Let them just soften through without coloring, then flip them over and repeat on the other side.

Meanwhile, mix your halloumi sticks, mint, oregano, and lemon juice together and set aside. Once the eggplant slices are softened and cool enough to handle, wrap each piece of halloumi in a slice of eggplant and secure with a toothpick. Keep the bowl of marinade for later.

Transfer to the barbecue and grill for 2–3 minutes on each side, until the eggplant is nicely charred and cooked through.

Add the extra virgin olive oil to the bowl containing the remaining herb and lemon juice marinade. Once the stuffed eggplant rolls are ready, transfer them to a serving platter and pour the lemon and herb dressing over the top. Serve hot.

Note: If you want to prepare these ahead, you can soften the eggplant slices on a baking sheet in a hot oven first, being careful not to let them color. Follow the instructions up to the end of marination, then cool and refrigerate them until you're ready to barbecue, or finish on a hot griddle pan.

CAULIFLOWER & CABBAGE

Technically brassicas, but who calls them that?
A lovely textural contrast for your barbecue.

**SPICED BUTTER CAULIFLOWER
WITH MARINATED FETA & LEMON   136**

**SMOKED RED CABBAGE WITH APPLES,
RAISINS & PECANS   140**

**CRISPY GINGER CAULIFLOWER WINGS
WITH TAMARIND & CILANTRO (VEGAN)   142**

**BARBECUED SPROUTS WITH CHILI,
LEMON & ALMONDS (VEGAN)   144**

**CRISPY CABBAGE
WITH CHILI SAGE BREADCRUMBS (VEGAN)   146**

SPICED BUTTER CAULIFLOWER
WITH MARINATED FETA & LEMON

While I enjoy the restrained drama of a whole cauliflower, carved at the table, you can reduce the time between prep and consumption by cutting your cauliflower into large steaks. This version with spiced butter and marinated feta is a favorite.

Serves: 4
Prep: 15 minutes
Cook: 25 minutes

1 large cauliflower, plus its leaves
8 cardamom pods, seeds only
2 teaspoons coriander seeds
2 tablespoons melted butter
1 teaspoon sea salt flakes
1 teaspoon red pepper flakes
1 tablespoon olive oil

FOR THE MARINATED FETA
7 ounces (200 g) feta, cut into
    small pieces
3 tablespoons extra virgin olive oil
½ lemon, juice only
3 pieces of lemon peel
A pinch of red pepper flakes
1 teaspoon coriander seeds,
    crushed
A handful of fresh mint leaves,
    roughly chopped

Trim the base of the cauliflower, then carefully slice it into 1-inch (2½ cm) "steaks"—you should have at least 4. (Save the trimmings and roast them with a little oil, sea salt, and smoked paprika to have as a snack.)

Crush the cardamom and coriander seeds with a mortar and pestle, then mix with the melted butter, sea salt flakes, and red pepper flakes. Brush the mixture all over the cauliflower steaks, toss the cauliflower leaves with the olive oil, and set both aside.

Gently stir the feta with the olive oil, lemon juice, lemon peel, red pepper flakes, coriander seeds, and mint and set aside.

Once your barbecue is good and hot, grill the cauliflower steaks for 10 minutes on one side and 5–8 minutes on the other side, until nicely charred and just cooked through. When your cauliflower has about 10 minutes left, grill the reserved leaves for 2–3 minutes or until crisp.

Arrange the steaks and leaves on a platter and top with the marinated feta and dressing. Serve hot.

SMOKED RED CABBAGE WITH APPLES, RAISINS & PECANS

You'll get maximum flavor in this dish using a charcoal barbecue and a good handful of dry twigs—I like to use apple or plum. The smoke infuses into the cabbage and makes a filling salad.

Serves: 4
Prep: 15 minutes
Cook: 20 minutes

1 red cabbage,
   cut into eighths,
   leaves separated
2 tablespoons olive oil
1 teaspoon sea salt flakes
1 Pink Lady apple, cored
   and cut into eighths
3½ ounces (100 g) raisins
3½ ounces (100 g) pecans

FOR THE DRESSING
⅓ ounce (10 g) fresh chives,
   finely chopped
⅔ cup (150 ml) sour cream or yogurt
½ lemon, juice only
A pinch of sea salt flakes

Toss the cabbage leaves, olive oil, and sea salt flakes in a large bowl until the leaves are evenly coated. Once your barbecue is good and hot, grill the leaves for 3–4 minutes on each side, until cooked through—you can let them crisp up and char, or take them off just before they start to catch.

Meanwhile, mix together the chives, sour cream or yogurt, lemon juice, and sea salt flakes, tasting and adjusting the seasoning as needed.

Pile the cooked and charred leaves onto a large platter, top with the apples, raisins, and pecans, and serve warm with the sour cream dressing.

Note: If you prefer, you can let the cooked leaves cool a little, then roll them up and shred them—easier to spoon up with just a fork.

CRISPY GINGER CAULIFLOWER WINGS WITH TAMARIND & CILANTRO

These cauliflower wings are ridiculously moreish, and the sauce—made with store–bought jarred tamarind—couldn't be easier. Double up the quantities for a crowd.

Serves: 4 as a snack
Prep: 10 minutes
Cook: 10 minutes

1 large cauliflower, cut into small
   florets, plus its leaves
2 tablespoons olive or neutral oil
2 teaspoons ground ginger
   or grated fresh ginger
1 teaspoon sea salt flakes
A handful of fresh cilantro,
   chopped

FOR THE DRESSING
1 ounce (30 g) tamarind paste, from
   a jar (not tamarind concentrate)
1 tablespoon olive oil

Combine the cauliflower florets and leaves in a large bowl with the oil, ginger, and sea salt flakes. Mix well until everything is evenly coated.

Once your barbecue is good and hot, cook the florets for 3–4 minutes on each side, until charred and cooked through; the leaves will take about 2 minutes per side.

In the bowl you used for the cauliflower, mix the tamarind paste and the olive oil to make the dressing. Taste and add salt if needed—most supermarket tamarind paste is salted, so you probably won't need any. As soon as the cauliflower florets and leaves are cooked, add them to the bowl with the dressing and toss to coat.

Arrange the cauliflower on a serving dish, top with the chopped cilantro, and serve hot.

BARBECUED SPROUTS WITH CHILI, LEMON & ALMONDS

Sprouts on a barbecue? They remind me very much of chestnuts and to my mind only benefit from a quick blast on the coals. Dressed with punchy chili and lemon, these are an exceptional side.

Serves: 4 as a side
Prep: 10 minutes
Cook: 10 minutes tops

7 ounces (200 g) large Brussels sprouts, halved (leave the small ones whole)
2 tablespoons olive oil
1 teaspoon sea salt flakes
1¾ ounces (50 g) toasted flaked almonds
A handful of fresh flat-leaf parsley, roughly chopped

FOR THE DRESSING
1 fresh red chili, finely chopped
1 lemon, zest and juice
2 tablespoons extra virgin olive oil
1 teaspoon sea salt flakes

Mix the halved and whole sprouts with the olive oil and sea salt flakes in a large bowl.

For the dressing, stir the chili, lemon zest and juice, olive oil, and sea salt together, taste and adjust the salt and lemon as needed, and set aside.

Once your barbecue is medium hot, cook the sprouts for 5–6 minutes on each side, until charred and just cooked through.

Dress the cooked sprouts with the lemon and chili dressing, and serve scattered with the flaked almonds and flat-leaf parsley.

CRISPY CABBAGE
WITH CHILI SAGE BREADCRUMBS

One of my favorite dishes in the book—cabbage is just glorious on the barbecue, crispy at the edges, gently steamed inside. With chili and sage through the crispy breadcrumbs, these are exceptional.

Serves: 4
Prep: 15 minutes
Cook: 15 minutes tops

1 sweetheart cabbage
2 tablespoons olive oil
1 teaspoon sea salt flakes

FOR THE SAGE BREADCRUMBS
3 tablespoons olive oil
10 fresh sage leaves, finely chopped
½ teaspoon red pepper flakes
A pinch of sea salt flakes
1¾ ounces (50 g) panko or white
  breadcrumbs
½ large lemon, juice only, to serve

Cut the cabbage into eighths, leaving the stem intact so the pieces stay together. Gently dress with the olive oil and sea salt, rubbing as much as possible into the cut surfaces and leaves.

Heat the oil in a frying pan over medium heat and add the sage leaves, red pepper flakes, and sea salt. Fry for 2–3 minutes, until the sage starts to color, then add the breadcrumbs. Lower the heat and stir occasionally for 5–6 minutes, until the crumbs are evenly golden brown. Let the breadcrumbs cool (easy to forget), then taste and add salt as needed.

Once your barbecue is medium to hot, grill the cabbage for 6–8 minutes per side, until just charred and cooked through. (If you stick a fork into the cabbage, it should yield easily.)

Pile the cabbage onto a platter, dress with the lemon juice, scatter with the sage breadcrumbs, and serve hot.

Note: Keep any leftover breadcrumbs to scatter over hot pasta or a gratin.

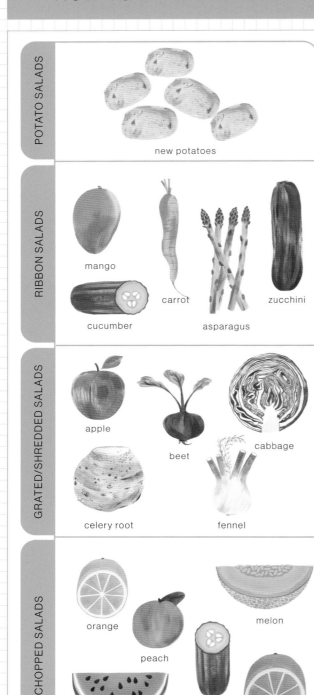

POTATO SALADS

new potatoes

RIBBON SALADS

mango

carrot

asparagus

zucchini

cucumber

GRATED/SHREDDED SALADS

apple

beet

cabbage

celery root

fennel

CHOPPED SALADS

orange

peach

melon

watermelon

cucumber

grapefruit

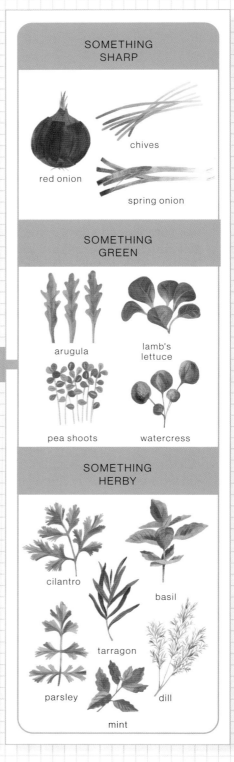

SOMETHING SHARP

red onion

chives

spring onion

SOMETHING GREEN

arugula

lamb's lettuce

pea shoots

watercress

SOMETHING HERBY

cilantro

basil

tarragon

parsley

dill

mint

THE ALL-IMPORTANT DRESSING BASE

OLIVE & LEMON DRESSING

 1 tablespoon extra virgin olive oil

 1 lemon, juice only

 ½ teaspoon sea salt flakes

SESAME & LIME DRESSING

 1 tablespoon sesame oil

 1 lime, juice only

 ½ teaspoon sea salt flakes

VINEGAR DRESSING

 1 tablespoon extra virgin olive oil

 1 tablespoon red or white wine vinegar

 ½ teaspoon sea salt flakes

SESAME SOY DRESSING

 1 tablespoon sesame oil

 1 tablespoon rice wine vinegar

 1 tablespoon soy sauce

SOMETHING HOT

harissa

Dijon mustard

ground black pepper

chili

PERHAPS DAIRY

yogurt

mayonnaise

SOMETHING CRUNCHY

peanuts

walnuts

almonds

pecans

hazelnuts

AND MAYBE CHEESE

feta

goat cheese

blue cheese

mozzarella

POTATO SALADS

750G WAXY/NEW POTATOES
(RED BLISS, PEE WEES,
FINGERLINGS, ETC.)

Boil in salted water until tender, halve,
then combine as shown on pages 148–149.

RIBBON SALADS

A COMBINATION OF YOUR CHOICE
OF MANGO, CARROT, CUCUMBER,
ASPARAGUS, OR ZUCCHINI

Slice into ribbons using a peeler,
then combine as shown on pages 148–149.

GRATED/SHREDDED SALADS

A COMBINATION OF YOUR CHOICE
OF FENNEL, BEETS, APPLES,
CELERY ROOT, OR CABBAGE

Grate using a box grater, grating attachment of
your food processor, or thinly slice,
then combine as shown on pages 148–149.

CHOPPED SALADS

A COMBINATION OF YOUR CHOICE
OF CUCUMBER, PEACH, MELON,
GRAPEFRUIT, ORANGE, OR WATERMELON

Chop or slice into large chunks,
then combine as shown on pages 148–149.

AVOCADO THREE WAYS

MANGO & AVOCADO SALSA

1 avocado, just underripe, cut into ⅕-inch (½ cm) cubes

1 mango, just underripe, cut into ⅕-inch (½ cm) cubes

½ pomegranate, seeds only

1 fresh red chili, finely chopped

2 limes, zest and juice

¾ ounce (20 g) fresh basil leaves, torn

sea salt flakes, to taste

Serves: 4 generously
Prep time: 15 minutes

Mix everything together, then taste and adjust the salt. Serve at room temperature—you can make this a few hours ahead and chill until needed.

TOMATO & RED ONION GUACAMOLE

3 ripe avocados

½ red onion, very finely chopped

1 small tomato, finely chopped

¾ ounce (20 g) fresh cilantro, finely chopped

2 teaspoons sea salt flakes

2 limes, juice only

Serves: 6 generously
Prep time: 15 minutes

Roughly chop or mash the avocado flesh, then mix with the onion, tomato, and cilantro. Add lime juice and sea salt flakes to taste.

GRAPEFRUIT, AVOCADO & PINEAPPLE SALSA

ALL VEGAN

1 avocado, just underripe, cut into ⅓-inch (1 cm) cubes

1 grapefruit, cut into ⅓-inch (1 cm) cubes

½ fresh pineapple, cut into ⅕-inch (½ cm) cubes

¾ ounce (20 g) fresh mint, finely chopped

2 limes, juice only

1 teaspoon sea salt flakes

Serves: 6 generously
Prep time: 15 minutes

Mix the avocado, grapefruit, pineapple, mint, lime juice, and sea salt flakes together just before you're ready to eat. Adjust the salt and serve.

SOUR CREAM THREE WAYS

Serves: 4
Prep: 10 minutes

1¼ cups (300 ml) sour
cream or natural yogurt

Stir the sour cream or yogurt in a bowl with your chosen variation ingredients, then taste and adjust the salt as needed. Serve at room temperature—you can make these a few hours ahead and chill before bringing them out as needed.

ROASTED GARLIC TZATZIKI

3 garlic cloves

¼ cucumber,
seeds removed, grated

½ tablespoon
olive oil

sea salt flakes,
to taste

Roast the garlic with the olive oil for 20 minutes at 400°F (200°C)—ideally alongside another dish in the oven so you aren't turning it on just for the garlic. I often make an entire trayful from 2 or 3 bulbs of garlic with a generous amount of olive oil, then peel and store them in the fridge for future use.

Squeeze out the roasted garlic and mix it with the sour cream and grated cucumber. Add sea salt flakes to taste and serve.

SPRING ONION & LIME

6 spring onions,
finely chopped

1 lime,
zest and juice

sea salt flakes, to taste

BLUE CHEESE & CHIVE

3½ ounces (100 g) blue
cheese, crumbled

⅓ ounce (10 g) chives,
finely chopped

sea salt flakes, to taste

CHARRED EGGPLANT THREE WAYS

CHILI, RED ONION & CILANTRO

3 eggplants, whole

½ red onion, very finely chopped

1 large lemon, juice only

1 teaspoon sea salt flakes

1 ounce (30 g) fresh cilantro, chopped

½ teaspoon chili flakes

1 teaspoon ground roasted cumin

2 tablespoons olive oil

HARISSA & POMEGRANATE

3 eggplants, whole

½ pomegranate, seeds only

2–3 teaspoons harissa paste

1 ounce (30 g) fresh mint, chopped

1 large lemon, juice only

2 tablespoons olive oil

1 teaspoon sea salt flakes

CHARRED TOMATOES & LIME

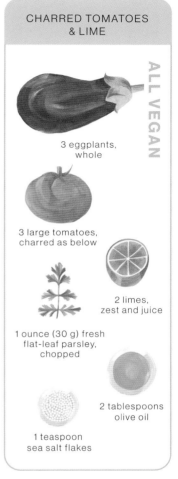

ALL VEGAN

3 eggplants, whole

3 large tomatoes, charred as below

2 limes, zest and juice

1 ounce (30 g) fresh flat-leaf parsley, chopped

2 tablespoons olive oil

1 teaspoon sea salt flakes

Serves: 4
Prep: 15 minutes
Cook: 30–40 minutes

Place the eggplants directly on the hot coals of your barbecue and turn them after about 20 minutes. You want the skin to completely blacken, and when you insert a knife, the insides should feel soft, as if the eggplant has collapsed from the inside. Alternatively, you can do this under a scorchingly hot grill for 15 minutes on each side. Let the burnt eggplants cool down a bit, and once you're able to handle them, halve and scoop out the flesh.

Mash the flesh in a bowl with your chosen variation ingredients. Think of this like making a pesto: you're adding salt, oil, and lemon or lime juice to taste, so follow the recipe, then taste and adjust until you are happy with the flavor.

If you are making the variation with charred tomatoes, brush the whole tomatoes with oil and place on a hot barbecue to grill for 7–8 minutes on each side. You can do the same indoors under a very hot grill.

NAAN THREE WAYS

GARLIC, CORIANDER & CUMIN

2 garlic cloves, grated or crushed

1 tablespoon coriander seeds, crushed

1 tablespoon cumin seeds, crushed

BEET & CUMIN

3½ ounces (100 g) grated beet

1 tablespoon cumin seeds, crushed

POMEGRANATE & CILANTRO

3 tablespoons pomegranate seeds

3 tablespoons chopped fresh cilantro

1 tablespoon nigella seeds

Makes:	4 naan breads
Prep:	15 minutes,
	plus 1 hour resting
Cook:	3 minutes

2½ cups (300 g) plain flour
1 teaspoon baking powder
1 teaspoon sea salt flakes
1 teaspoon sugar
1 tablespoon melted butter
   (or ghee), plus extra for brushing
1 cup (200 ml) milk

Mix together the flour, baking powder, sea salt flakes, sugar, and butter, and gradually work in the milk until you have a stiff dough, adding in your variation ingredients as detailed above. Knead for 5–10 minutes. Cover in an oiled bowl, then leave to rest for 1–2 hours.

Once your barbecue is good and hot, divide the dough into 4 equal pieces. Roll the dough out into circles about the size of a large saucer, then pull each into a teardrop shape. Leave them to rest for 5 minutes.

Brush the barbecue grill with butter, then cook the bread for about 1–1½ minutes on each side, until blackened in spots and cooked through. Brush with more butter and serve warm.

Cook indoors: Heat your grill to a medium-high setting and preheat a heavy baking sheet. Arrange the pieces on the hot baking sheet and grill for 2–3 minutes, until cooked through.

FLATBREAD THREE WAYS

FIG, FETA & FENNEL

2 fresh figs,
chopped

3½ ounces (100 g) feta cheese,
crumbled

2 teaspoons
fennel seeds

WALNUT & HERB

2 ounces (60 g) walnuts,
finely chopped

1½ ounces (40 g) finely chopped
soft fresh herbs
(cilantro, parsley, etc.)

PEAR, RICOTTA & HONEY

2 small firm pears,
grated

6 tablespoons   6 teaspoons
ricotta   honey

A pinch of freshly ground
black pepper

Serves: 4–6
Prep: 5–10 minutes, plus 1 hour resting
Cook: 2–4 minutes

⅓ cup (75 ml) olive oil
1 teaspoon sea salt flakes
1 cup (200 ml) warm water
1 teaspoon honey
3⅓ cups (400 g) strong white bread flour
1 teaspoon fast-acting dried yeast

Mix all the base dough ingredients together and knead for 5–10 minutes, until smooth. Transfer the dough to an oiled bowl, cover, and leave to rise for 1 hour or until doubled in size.

Punch down the dough, then for the first two varations, knead through your chosen flavors, using a little flour if the dough becomes too sticky. Divide the dough into 6 pieces and roll each into 8-inch (20 cm) rounds.

Brush your barbecue with oil and cook the flatbreads on a medium-hot grill for 2–4 minutes per side, until just cooked through and charred. Serve hot.

For the pear, ricotta, and honey flatbreads, squeeze the excess water from the grated pear. Divide the dough into 6 pieces and, on a floured surface, roll each piece into a circle the size of a side plate.

Scatter a tablespoon of ricotta and pear in the center, leaving a 1½-inch (4 cm) border around the edges, and drizzle with a teaspoon of honey and a little freshly ground black pepper. Fold three sides of your dough in and gently pat down into a triangle, rolling very gently to enclose the filling.

Cook indoors: You can bake these in the oven for 8–10 minutes at 450°F (230°C).

TAKE IT TO THE BEACH (OR PARK)

PORTABLE BARBECUE FOOD—JUST PACK IT
ALL UP AND STICK IT ON A SMALL BARBECUE
WHEN YOU GET THERE.

TAKE IT TO THE BEACH (OR PARK)

EGGPLANT & GOAT CHEESE BURGER STACKS
WITH HONEY & THYME   166

RED PEPPER, FETA, BASIL
& PINE NUT PARCELS   170

SIMPLE SAGE & ONION CANNELLINI
BURGERS (VEGAN)   172

CHIPOTLE MUSHROOM & BLACK BEAN BURGERS
WITH PEANUTS & LIME (VEGAN)   174

LEEK & CHEDDAR GLAMORGAN SAUSAGES   176

SZECHUAN EGGPLANT WEDGES
WITH BLACK BEAN SAUCE (VEGAN)   178

LIME PICKLE, BUTTERNUT SQUASH
& HALLOUMI BURGERS   180

TANDOORI FENNEL STEAKS WITH MINT RAITA   184

LIME & CHILI CORN FRITTERS
WITH ROASTED TOMATOES   186

CHILI CHEESE FRENCH-TOASTED CRUMPETS
WITH SAGE   188

SECRET GARDEN WHOLE ROASTED EGGS
& NEW POTATOES WITH SALSA VERDE   190

EGGPLANT & GOAT CHEESE BURGER STACKS WITH HONEY & THYME

One of my favorite Spanish dishes is berenjenas con miel—eggplant, deep-fried in batter, served with honey. It occurred to me that goat cheese is just as lovely with honey as eggplant, and so these moreish burger stacks were born. The cheese melts between the eggplant slices, scented with thyme—perfect by themselves or squashed between crusty white rolls.

Serves: 4
Prep: 10 minutes
Cook: 30 minutes

2 large, evenly sized eggplants
Two 3½-ounce (100 g) wheels
  goat cheese with rind
A handful of fresh lemon thyme
  sprigs
Olive oil, for brushing
Sea salt flakes
Freshly ground black pepper
Clear honey
Crusty rolls, to serve

Cut the eggplants into ⅓-inch (1 cm) slices and the goat cheese into very thin rounds. Sandwich each piece of goat cheese between two similarly sized slices of eggplant along with a sprig of thyme. Brush both sides of the eggplant with oil and add a tiny pinch of sea salt flakes and black pepper.

Once your barbecue is ready, place the eggplant stacks on the grill and cook for 10–15 minutes per side, until the eggplant is cooked through and the cheese has melted. You can flip them every 5–6 minutes or so and give them a brush with olive oil.

Transfer to a serving platter, drizzle with honey, top with the remaining thyme, and serve with crusty rolls on the side.

RED PEPPER, FETA, BASIL & PINE NUT PARCELS

In this recipe, I use the cut halves of red peppers to hold the filling, so what you get is somewhere between a supersized stuffed pepper and a squashable, melted-cheese-filled burger. It reminds me of a scene in *The Godfather,* where a mobster fries up red peppers to make a simple but delicious sandwich.

Serves: 4
Prep: 15 minutes
Cook: 30 minutes

4 red peppers, halved
  and deseeded
Olive oil for brushing
1¾ ounces (50 g) pine nuts
7 ounces (200 g) feta cheese,
  crumbled
1 lemon, zest and juice
A handful of fresh basil, chopped
1 fresh red chili, chopped
Burger buns (optional)

Brush both sides of the halved peppers with a little olive oil. Once your barbecue is medium hot, barbecue the peppers for about 10 minutes on each side, until charred and slightly softened.

Mix together the pine nuts, feta cheese, lemon zest and juice, chopped basil, and chopped chili.

Remove the softened peppers and stuff 4 of the halves with the feta and basil mixture. Lay the other 4 pepper halves on top and return them to the barbecue for a further 5 minutes on each side to warm the feta through.

Eat them as they are or stuff into burger buns.

SIMPLE SAGE & ONION CANNELLINI BURGERS

I used to use this combination as a filling for vegan sausage rolls and with a little experimentation came up with this version in burger form—perfect in rolls with a spoon of mustard on the side.

Serves: 6
Prep: 20 minutes
Cook: 30 minutes

7 ounces (200 g) small potatoes, whole
1 large white onion, roughly chopped
2 garlic cloves, whole
1 teaspoon freshly ground black pepper
1 teaspoon sea salt flakes
10 sage leaves, roughly chopped
1 tablespoon olive oil
One 15-ounce (425 g) can cannellini beans, drained well but not rinsed
2 teaspoons Dijon mustard
2 teaspoons cornstarch
6 burger buns, to serve

Place the potatoes, onion, garlic, pepper, salt, sage, and olive oil on a small baking sheet. Roast for 30 minutes at 400°F (200°C), until the potatoes are cooked through and the onions are soft.

Squeeze the garlic out from its skin, then pulse the vegetables together with the cannellini beans, mustard, and cornstarch in a food processor—you want the texture of a thick mash.

Taste the mixture and add salt as needed, then use tablespoons to form the mixture into 6 burger patties on a lined baking sheet.

Bake the burgers at 400°F (200°C) for 25–30 minutes, until golden brown and crisp. You can eat them immediately at this stage, or if packing them for a picnic, let them cool down, then give them a final blast for a couple of minutes per side on a hot, well-oiled barbecue just before serving.

CHIPOTLE MUSHROOM & BLACK BEAN BURGERS WITH PEANUTS & LIME

These burgers are ridiculously moreish—I like to serve them in buns with mayonnaise and pickles. Make life easier for yourself by cooking them in the oven first, then finishing them off with a quick grill on the barbecue before serving.

Serves: 4
Prep: 20 minutes
Cook: 25 minutes

1¾ ounces (50 g) smooth
    peanut butter
One 15-ounce (425 g) can black
    beans, drained but not rinsed
2 small garlic cloves
2 teaspoons red pepper flakes
1 teaspoon ground cumin
1 tablespoon olive oil
1 heaped tablespoon rye flour
1 lime, zest only
1 teaspoon sea salt flakes
9 ounces (250 g) button
mushrooms

TO SERVE
1 lime, cut into 4 wedges
A handful of chopped salted
    peanuts
A handful of chopped fresh
    cilantro
4 burger buns

Put the peanut butter into a food processor with 2 ounces (60 g) of the black beans, the garlic, red pepper flakes, cumin, olive oil, rye flour, lime zest, and sea salt flakes and blitz until you have a very thick paste. Pour into a large bowl and stir in the rest of the black beans.

Put the mushrooms in the processor—no need to clean it out—and pulse until you have a dry mushroom mince. Stir this into the black bean mixture. With damp hands, form the mixture into 4 thick burgers and arrange them on a lined baking sheet.

Bake in the oven at 400°F (200°C) for 25–30 minutes. When they've got 10 minutes left, gently flip them over so they can crisp up on the other side.

They're ready to serve straight from the oven, but for a nice bit of smokiness you can let them cool down, then finish them on a medium barbecue for a couple of minutes per side.

Squeeze the lime wedges on the burgers and top with a handful of chopped peanuts and cilantro, then sandwich them into lightly grilled burger buns.

LEEK & CHEDDAR GLAMORGAN SAUSAGES

These are inspired by the classic Welsh Glamorgan sausages, adapted for the barbecue with three of my favorite ingredients: Cheddar, mustard, and sage. You can mostly cook these in advance in the oven and finish them off on the barbecue—perfect to transport to the park or beach.

Serves: 4 generously
Prep: 30 minutes,
             plus 1 hour chilling
Cook: 30 minutes

2 tablespoons olive oil, plus more for
    brushing
2 leeks, thinly sliced
1 teaspoon sea salt flakes
5 ounces (150 g) Cheddar, grated
1 heaped teaspoon mustard
10 sage leaves, finely chopped
2 free-range egg yolks
3½ ounces (100 g) fresh white
    breadcrumbs
1 teaspoon freshly ground
    black pepper
Plain flour, for shaping
4 hot dog buns and mustard,
    for serving

Heat the oil in a medium saucepan, add the leeks and sea salt flakes, then stir, cover, and soften for 10 minutes over low heat, stirring occasionally. Once the leeks have softened, let them cool down, then press them between a few sheets of paper towel to remove any excess moisture.

Mix the leeks with the grated cheese, mustard, sage, egg yolks, breadcrumbs, and black pepper. With lightly floured hands, form the mixture into 8 small sausages and put them on a floured plate. Cover and chill for at least an hour or overnight.

Preheat the oven to 400°F (200°C). Transfer the sausages to a lined baking sheet, brush them with olive oil, and bake for 30 minutes. Then finish them off on the barbecue for a few minutes on each side to char.

Serve in hot dog buns, two sausages to each bun, with more mustard.

SZECHUAN EGGPLANT WEDGES WITH BLACK BEAN SAUCE

Eggplants cooked with black bean sauce are ridiculously tasty. Serve them alongside a range of other Southeast Asian-inspired dishes (see pages 60, 98, and 100) for a themed barbecue.

Serves: 4
Prep: 15 minutes
Cook: 15 minutes

3 tablespoons black bean sauce
1 tablespoon sesame oil
2 eggplants, cut into ¾-inch (2 cm) slices

FOR THE DRESSING
2 tablespoons sesame oil
1 tablespoon rice vinegar
4 spring onions, thinly sliced
1 fresh red chili, thinly sliced
1 garlic clove, finely chopped or grated
One 2-inch (5 cm) piece fresh ginger, finely chopped or grated
1 teaspoon granulated sugar

Mix the black bean sauce with the sesame oil in a large bowl, then gently stir through the eggplant slices until evenly coated.

Once your barbecue is good and hot, cook the eggplant slices for 6–7 minutes per side, until lightly charred and cooked through.

For the dressing, mix the sesame oil, vinegar, spring onions, chili, garlic, ginger, and sugar. (The black bean sauce has a lot of salt in it, so there's no extra salt in the dressing.)

Once the eggplant is done, arrange the slices on a platter and drizzle with the dressing. Taste and adjust the seasoning, if needed, and serve hot.

LIME PICKLE, BUTTERNUT SQUASH & HALLOUMI BURGERS

This is a wonderful flavor combination, with sweetness from the squash, depth from the halloumi, and a secret ingredient—lime pickle, inspired by Laura Goodman's cheese straws in her fantastic cookbook, *Carbs*. These are perfect to part-cook in the oven, then crisp up on the barbecue.

Serves: 6
Prep: 20 minutes
Cook: 30 minutes

1 pound (450 g) squash
4½ ounces (125 g) halloumi, grated
2½ ounces (75 g) lime pickle,
   roughly chopped
1 free-range egg, beaten
1 ounce (30 g) panko breadcrumbs
Olive oil, for brushing

TO SERVE
Yogurt
Toasted burger buns

Preheat the oven to 400°F (200°C). Peel, deseed, and grate the squash—you should be left with 12 ounces (350 g). Place in a clean tea towel, then twist into a tight ball and squeeze out as much liquid as you can. Mix it well with the grated halloumi, lime pickle, egg, and breadcrumbs, then form into 6 patties and put them on a lined baking tray. If you have time, put the baking tray into the fridge and chill for 30 minutes to an hour before cooking.

Transfer to the oven and bake for 20 minutes. At this point, you can take them out, let them cool down, pack and refrigerate them, then finish them off on a hot barbecue (make sure to oil the barbecue grill beforehand) for 2–3 minutes each side, until slightly charred and warmed through.

Serve with a dollop of yogurt and toasted burger buns.

TANDOORI FENNEL STEAKS WITH MINT RAITA

Fennel cut into thick steaks benefits from a longer cook over a low heat: it concentrates the sweetness. I like to make something that requires a quick flash grill over high heat first (like the Spiced Parmesan Corn with Lemon & Mint on page 128), and then add these once the coals have cooled to medium.

Serves: 4
Prep: 15 minutes
Cook: 20 minutes

2 round bulbs of fennel
1 teaspoon ground coriander
1 teaspoon ground cumin
1 teaspoon smoked paprika
½ teaspoon ground turmeric
½ teaspoon chili powder
1 teaspoon sea salt flakes
2 tablespoons olive oil

FOR THE RAITA
4 tablespoons natural yogurt
¼ cucumber, seeds removed,
   grated
½ small garlic clove, grated
1 teaspoon ground cumin
A pinch of sea salt flakes

TO SERVE
A handful of fresh mint leaves,
   roughly chopped
Flatbreads

Slice the fennel lengthwise into ½-inch (1½ cm) steaks, leaving the stem intact to help hold them together. Mix the spices, sea salt flakes, and oil in a bowl, then gently turn the fennel steaks in the spice mix until evenly coated.

Mix the yogurt, cucumber, garlic, cumin, and sea salt flakes together for the raita. Taste and adjust the salt as needed and set aside.

Once your barbecue is medium hot, cook the fennel steaks for 8–10 minutes on each side, until lightly charred and soft all the way through. (You can cover with a lid or an upside-down roasting pan if you wish.)

Top the fennel steaks with the fresh mint and serve with the raita and flatbreads alongside.

LIME & CHILI CORN FRITTERS WITH ROASTED TOMATOES

This is a version of a dish created originally for this book, adapted for BBC Food with canned corn during COVID-19, and adapted back again with corn on the cob—too nice not to include.

Serves: 4
Prep: 15 minutes
Cook: 30 minutes

4 ears corn on the cob
3 spring onions, thinly sliced
⅔ cup (75 g) plain flour
1 teaspoon ground cumin
1 teaspoon ground coriander
1 teaspoon smoked paprika
1 teaspoon sea salt flakes
1 fresh red chili, finely chopped
3½ ounces (100 g) natural yogurt
1 free-range egg, beaten
2 limes, zest and juice

FOR THE ROASTED TOMATOES
10½ ounces (300 g) cherry
    tomatoes on the vine
1 tablespoon olive oil
1 teaspoon sea salt flakes

Stand the corn upright on a chopping board and, using a sharp knife, slice the kernels off each side.

Put the kernels into a large bowl with the spring onions, flour, spices, sea salt flakes, and chili, then add the yogurt, egg, and the zest and juice of 1 lime, and stir until you have a thick batter.

Put the cherry tomatoes with their vines, oil, and sea salt into the middle of a piece of foil the size of a chopping board and fold it together into a neat parcel with the seam at the top. Place the foil packet directly on the coals (or on the grill if using a gas barbecue) and cook for 30 minutes.

Remove the tomatoes from the foil, discard the liquid, and mash the tomatoes into a thick sauce. Taste and adjust the salt as needed.

To start in the oven and finish on the barbecue: Drop heaped tablespoons of batter onto a lined baking sheet and flatten. Bake at 400°F (200°C) for 20 minutes, then finish the fritters on the barbecue, grilling them until crisp and golden brown.

Serve the fritters hot with the remaining lime juice and zest, and the roasted tomato sauce alongside.

CHILI CHEESE FRENCH-TOASTED CRUMPETS WITH SAGE

I love French toast and I love crumpets, and this version with sage, Cheddar, and chili is an indulgent snack. Serve for brunch late-morning or as an afternoon snack.

Serves: 3–6
Prep: 10 minutes
Cook: 10 minutes

3 medium free-range eggs,
   lightly beaten
3 tablespoons yogurt
3½ ounces (100 g) Cheddar, grated
1 fresh red chili, finely chopped
20 fresh sage leaves, chopped
½ teaspoon sea salt flakes
6 crumpets
Freshly ground black pepper,
   to serve

Whisk the eggs, yogurt, Cheddar, chili, sage, and sea salt flakes together in a large bowl. Gently stir through your crumpets to thoroughly coat them in the mixture, letting them soak for 5–10 minutes if you have time.

When your barbecue is good and hot, fish the crumpets out of the bowl and place them on the well-oiled grill, bubbly side up. Spoon over any remaining cheese and egg mixture, grill for 3–4 minutes, then flip over and cook for a further 2–3 minutes, until the egg has just set. Serve immediately with freshly ground black pepper.

Note: For a portable version, pack the egg mixture and crumpets separately, then dip the crumpets into the mixture and barbecue them to order. Of course, you can also cook these in a frying pan.

SECRET GARDEN WHOLE ROASTED EGGS
& NEW POTATOES WITH SALSA VERDE

I loved *The Secret Garden* growing up, particularly when the children start experimenting with outdoor cooking to avoid suspicion at dinner-time, as their appetites have grown thanks to their illicit gardening. I may have misremembered, but at one point I'm certain they cook eggs and potatoes whole on the embers of a fire outside. This dish, with a vibrant green salsa verde on the side, is my homage.

Serves: 4
Prep: 15 minutes
Cook: 30 minutes

1.3 pounds (600 g) new potatoes
2 tablespoons olive oil
1 teaspoon sea salt flakes
4 free-range eggs, whole

FOR THE SALSA VERDE
1 ounce (30 g) fresh flat-leaf parsley, finely chopped
A handful of fresh cilantro leaves, finely chopped
½ garlic clove, grated
3 tablespoons extra virgin olive oil
1 tablespoon red wine vinegar
1 teaspoon Dijon mustard
A pinch of sea salt flakes

Boil the new potatoes for 7–8 minutes, until just cooked through. Drain well, then stir through the olive oil and sea salt flakes.

For the salsa verde, stir the parsley, cilantro, garlic, olive oil, vinegar, Dijon, and sea salt flakes together. Taste and adjust the vinegar and salt as needed and set aside.

Once your barbecue is medium hot, place the potatoes and the eggs on it, putting the eggs on the cooler side of the barbecue (see page 11). Grill the potatoes for 10 minutes per side, until nicely golden brown and charred. Turn the eggs every 5 minutes so they cook evenly—this should take 20–25 minutes.

Dip the eggs in cold water, peel and halve them, then pile them on a plate with the crisp potatoes. Serve hot with the salsa verde.

SOMETHING SWEET

FINISH YOUR OUTDOOR FEAST WITH FRESH GRILLED FRUIT DRIZZLED IN INDULGENT MELTED CHOCOLATE, CARAMEL, OR PEANUT BUTTER (OR ALL THREE).

SOMETHING SWEET

SIMPLY ROASTED APRICOTS
WITH ROSE & PISTACHIO (VEGAN)   196

SAFFRON PEARS & RHUBARB WITH RICOTTA   198

THE ELVIS AFTERNOON BARBECUE SANDWICH:
CHOCOLATE, PEANUT BUTTER
& BANANA (VEGAN)   200

SUMMER PUDDING PACKETS:
VANILLA–ROASTED BERRIES WITH BRIOCHE,
MASCARPONE & ALMONDS   202

DULCE DE LECHE PASSION FRUIT POTS
WITH CHOCOLATE & RICOTTA   204

ORANGE FLOWER WATER PEACHES
WITH ROSEMARY, ALMONDS & CREAM   206

CINNAMON GRILLED PINEAPPLE
WITH TOASTED COCONUT (VEGAN)   210

HONEY & ORANGE GRILLED PAPAYA
WITH MINT   212

SIMPLY ROASTED APRICOTS
WITH ROSE & PISTACHIO

When you've had your fill of ripe apricots (which may take some time—every time I looked for them in the kitchen to make this dish, one or two had mysteriously disappeared from the fruit bowl), try them simply grilled on the barbecue with a lovely orange and rose dressing.

Serves: 4
Prep: 10 minutes
Cook: 10 minutes

8 just ripe apricots, halved
  and pits removed
Olive oil, for brushing
1 ounce (30 g) pistachios,
  roughly chopped
2 tablespoons dried rose petals
  (optional)
Demerara sugar, to serve

FOR THE DRESSING
1–2 drops of rosewater
½ orange, zest and juice
2 teaspoons granulated sugar

Brush the cut side of the apricots with a little olive oil.

For the dressing, mix the rosewater with the orange zest and juice and sugar, stirring until the sugar has dissolved. Go very gently with the rosewater—it varies in strength, and you want to use it drop by drop until you've reached the optimum level of rosiness, as Nigella Lawson says.

Once your barbecue is medium hot, barbecue the apricots cut side down for about 5 minutes or until just starting to char.

Tumble the fruit onto a plate and gently mix in the rose and orange dressing. Top with the pistachios and rose petals (if using), and serve warm, with the demerara sugar on the side for an optional sweet hit.

SAFFRON PEARS & RHUBARB WITH RICOTTA

I made this dish for my Dutch publishers on a visit to my apartment just before COVID-19 kicked in—so at the time of writing, this was a nostalgic dish, as I made it the last time I entertained at home. It's a light, elegant end to a party.

Serves: 4
Prep: 15 minutes
Cook: 10 minutes

1 large pinch of good saffron
⅔ cup (150 ml) boiling water
¾ cup (150 g) granulated sugar
3 firm, round, ripe pears, cut into
    ⅕-inch (½ cm) slices
Olive oil, for brushing
12 stalks of rhubarb,
    forced if in season
4 tablespoons ricotta
A handful of toasted hazelnuts
A few fresh mint leaves

First, get your saffron syrup ready: steep your saffron in a couple tablespoons of the boiling water for 5 minutes, then give it a good smash with the back of a spoon to release the color and flavor. Pour the saffron water into a small saucepan with the rest of the water and the sugar, and heat gently until the sugar has dissolved. Set aside.

Once your barbecue is good and hot, arrange the coals so that one side is a little cooler (see page 11). Brush the sliced pears with a little olive oil and cook on the cooler end of the barbecue for about 5–6 minutes on each side, until just tender. Repeat with the rhubarb for about 3 minutes per side, taking the fruit over to the hotter side of the barbecue with tongs as needed.

Once both fruits are just cooked through but still holding their shape, transfer to a shallow roasting pan and cover with the saffron syrup. If you have time, leave them to sit for anything from 10 minutes to an hour.

Serve the fruit in four bowls with a scoop of ricotta, a handful of toasted hazelnuts, and mint leaves to garnish.

THE ELVIS AFTERNOON BARBECUE SANDWICH: CHOCOLATE, PEANUT BUTTER & BANANA

This is unashamedly calorie-loaded. I've given the quantities below for just one sandwich: multiply as needed. Also works well for breakfast.

Serves: 1
Prep: 10 minutes
Cook: 8 minutes

2 thick slices of good white bread
1 tablespoon peanut butter
1 banana, sliced into coins
¾ ounce (20 g) dark vegan
   chocolate, roughly chopped
A pinch of sea salt flakes

Spread one side of the bread with the peanut butter, then top with the banana coins, dark chocolate, and a scattering of sea salt flakes. Sandwich with the other piece of bread and press down.

Once your barbecue is medium hot, grill your sandwich for 2–4 minutes on each side, pressing it down with a spatula, until the bread is toasted to your liking. Serve hot.

Note: If you are vegan or making this for vegans, make sure to use vegan dark chocolate.

SUMMER PUDDING PACKETS:
VANILLA-ROASTED BERRIES
WITH BRIOCHE, MASCARPONE & ALMONDS

This deconstructed spin on a summer pudding (where deconstructed is code for much, much easier) lets you gently cook your fruit in a packet on the barbecue and toast your brioche alongside. Replace the chilled mascarpone with ice cream, if you wish.

Serves: 4
Prep: 10 minutes
Cook: 10 minutes

5 ounces (150 g) blackberries
10 ounces (275 g) raspberries
8 ounces (225 g) blueberries or
  grapes
2 teaspoons granulated sugar
1 vanilla pod, split
8 slices of brioche
4 tablespoons chilled mascarpone
A handful of toasted almonds
  and fresh mint leaves, to serve

Take a large piece of foil and place the blackberries, raspberries, and blueberries or grapes in the middle. Sprinkle the sugar and lay the vanilla pod on top, and then fold the foil into a neat parcel with the seam at the top.

Once your barbecue is medium hot, place the foil packet on one side of the barbecue and let the berries cook for 10–15 minutes. Meanwhile, toast your sliced brioche in batches on the other side of the barbecue, cutting them into triangles once toasted.

Divide the lightly cooked fruit between four plates with the toasted brioche. Add a tablespoon of mascarpone, top with the toasted almonds and mint leaves, and serve hot.

DULCE DE LECHE PASSION FRUIT POTS WITH CHOCOLATE & RICOTTA

I love the combination of passion fruit with chocolate: it works beautifully with dulce de leche in these easy, mildly addictive custard pots. Wheel a plate of these out with coffee after dinner—they're simple to prepare ahead and just flash on the barbecue to finish off.

Serves: 4–6
Prep: 10 minutes
Cook: 15 minutes

8 passion fruit, halved
2 ounces (60 g) ricotta
2 free-range egg yolks
1½ ounces (40 g) dulce de leche
  (or use tinned caramel)
A pinch of sea salt flakes
1 ounce (30 g) 70% dark chocolate,
  roughly chopped, plus 1 square for
  grating

Scoop the seeds and flesh from the passion fruit, reserving the shells, and transfer to a bowl with the ricotta, egg yolks, dulce de leche, and a pinch of sea salt flakes. Whisk until well incorporated.

Divide the chopped dark chocolate between the empty passion fruit shells, then fill each to the top with the caramel ricotta mixture.

Once your barbecue is medium hot, place the shells on the barbecue, filling side up. Cover with a lid or upside-down roasting pan and cook for 10–15 minutes, until the filling has set into a thick custard.

Grate over a little dark chocolate just before serving hot with teaspoons.

ORANGE FLOWER WATER PEACHES WITH ROSEMARY, ALMONDS & CREAM

Rosemary, sage, thyme—I love using them in sweet dishes, particularly with fruit. Here, rosemary combines with lightly grilled peaches and crisp almonds for an easy end to a late-summer party.

Serves: 4
Prep: 10 minutes
Cook: under 20 minutes

3 heaped tablespoons soft light brown sugar
2 sprigs of fresh rosemary, leaves finely chopped
4 just ripe to underripe peaches, halved
1½ ounces (40 g) toasted flaked almonds
2 teaspoons orange flower water
Crème fraîche, to serve

Mix the sugar and rosemary together and set aside on a plate.

Once your barbecue is ready, dip the cut side of the peaches in the rosemary sugar, then grill the peaches cut side up for 5 minutes. Flip them over and grill for a further 5 minutes, keeping a close eye so the sugar caramelizes rather than burns. (Don't worry if you lose a bit of sugar to the grill— the peaches will still caramelize beautifully.)

Remove the hot peaches from the grill and arrange on a platter. Sprinkle with the flaked almonds, top with the orange flower water, and serve hot with the crème fraîche alongside.

CINNAMON GRILLED PINEAPPLE WITH TOASTED COCONUT

At Dinner by Heston Blumenthal, pineapples are slow-cooked whole on a rotating spit—fun to watch and even more so to eat. You could certainly adapt the recipe below to cook the pineapple peeled and whole, turning it on the barbecue every 5 minutes or so and using the leaves as a handle. For a quicker version, slice it up and brush with this moreish cinnamon sugar glaze.

Serves: 4
Prep: 10 minutes
Cook: 15 minutes

2 tablespoons soft dark brown
  sugar
2 tablespoons water
1 teaspoon ground cinnamon
1 large pineapple, peeled, cored,
  and cut into eighths
1 lime, juice only
A handful of toasted coconut flakes
  and fresh mint leaves, to serve

Mix the dark brown sugar, water, and cinnamon together and set aside.

Once your barbecue is medium hot, grill the pineapple for 3–4 minutes on each side, until starting to catch. Brush generously with the cinnamon sugar mixture, then grill for a further 2 minutes or so on each side, until caramelized.

Arrange the pineapple on a platter and squeeze the lime juice on top. Sprinkle with the toasted coconut flakes and mint leaves, and serve hot.

HONEY & ORANGE GRILLED PAPAYA WITH MINT

A simple and refreshing end to a barbecue with a nice citrus kick. Serve with teaspoons to scoop out the insides as with a kiwi. I love the flavors you get from cooking half the citrus marinade on the barbecue and leaving the rest as a fresh dressing to finish.

Serves: 4
Prep: 10 minutes
Cook: 15 minutes

3 tablespoons olive or coconut oil
3 tablespoons honey
½ orange, juice and zest
1 lime, juice and zest
2 just ripe papayas, quartered,
   seeds removed
A handful of fresh mint leaves,
   to serve

Mix the olive or coconut oil, honey, orange and lime juice and zest together, then brush half over the cut sides of the papaya. Reserve the remaining mixture and set aside.

Once your barbecue is good and hot, cook the papaya cut side up for 5 minutes. Then flip and cook for another 3–5 minutes, until the sugars caramelize.

Pour the dressing over the hot papaya quarters and sprinkle with the fresh mint leaves before serving.

Note: To veganize, substitute maple syrup for the honey.

WHAT TO DO WITH
YOUR LEFTOVERS

WHAT TO DO WITH YOUR LEFTOVERS

BUILD A BANH MI   218

MAKE A RICE OR NOODLE BOWL   219

ADD IT TO PASTA   220

MAKE IT BREAKFAST   221

BUILD A BANH MI (VIETNAMESE BAGUETTE)

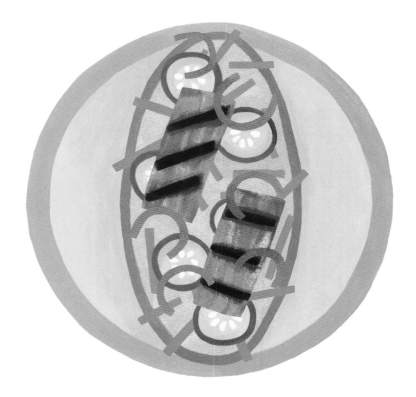

Grab yourself a baguette; some crisp, cold shredded carrots; cucumber; and cilantro (pickled mooli is optional) and build yourself the classic Vietnamese banh mi. Usually stuffed with marinated tofu or tempeh when vegetarian, you could equally use leftovers of any of the following recipes:

CHARRED ASPARAGUS WITH CHILI,
PEANUTS & COCONUT

GRILLED PAPAYA WITH TAMARIND,
CHILI & COCONUT

SRIRACHA-GRILLED TOFU
WITH SPRING ONIONS, LIME & CILANTRO

VIETNAMESE GRILLED TOFU
WITH TOMATOES & SPRING ONIONS

MAKE A RICE OR NOODLE BOWL

With leftovers from the recipes below, build yourself a Korean-inspired bibimbap bowl of rice with colorful toppings, or use them to top noodles and broth.

BARBECUED SPROUTS WITH CHILI,
LEMON & ALMONDS

CRISPY GINGER-CAULIFLOWER WINGS
WITH TAMARIND & CILANTRO

GUNPOWDER POTATOES WITH FENNEL SEEDS,
CHILI, CILANTRO & CASHEWS

SPICED PANEER WITH GRILLED MANGO,
AVOCADO, CHILI & CILANTRO

PANEER WITH HARISSA, GRILLED GREEN BEANS,
CHICKPEAS & LIME

ADD IT TO PASTA

The recipes below work beautifully chopped into bite-sized pieces, then added to a bowl of linguine or spaghetti for a hot lunch, or chilled penne, fusilli, or macaroni for the perfect lunchbox salad—just add along with a little good olive oil.

RED PEPPER, FETA, BASIL & PINE NUT BURGERS

SIMPLE SAGE & ONION CANNELLINI BURGERS

GRILLED PORTOBELLO MUSHROOMS
& LEEKS WITH TARRAGON & WALNUTS

RICOTTA WITH GRILLED SQUASH, CHARD,
HONEY & HAZELNUTS

GRILLED ASPARAGUS, RADISHES & BURRATA
WITH LEMON & BASIL

MAKE IT BREAKFAST

Leftover grilled fruit makes an excellent topping for porridge, granola with yogurt, or French toast. Use up the following:

HONEY & ORANGE GRILLED PAPAYA WITH MINT

SIMPLY ROASTED APRICOTS WITH ROSE & PISTACHIO

CINNAMON GRILLED PINEAPPLE WITH
TOASTED COCONUT

ORANGE FLOWER WATER PEACHES WITH
ROSEMARY, ALMONDS & CREAM

SUMMER PUDDING PACKETS: VANILLA-ROASTED BERRIES
WITH BRIOCHE, MASCARPONE & ALMONDS

GRILLED CHERRIES WITH WARM GOAT CHEESE,
MINT & WALNUTS (USE TO TOP BUTTERED MUFFINS
OR SAVORY FRENCH TOAST)

ACKNOWLEDGMENTS

I'd like to thank the team at Countryman Press for bringing this edition of the book together for the US market: Isabel McCarthy, for commissioning it and being lovely to work with from across the pond; production manager Devon Zahn; designer Allison Chi; managing editor Jess Murphy; publicist Rhina Garcia; and marketing manager Jessica Gilo. I'm so happy that *The Green Barbecue* is coming out in the United States with an imprint of W. W. Norton, particularly as I have fond memories of the giant Norton anthologies of literature from university.

The idea for a vegetarian barbecue book came from *The Roasting Tin* series UK editor Rowan Yapp, and I'd like to thank her for her continued support and friendship. Thanks to Felicity Blunt, for her wonderful agenting and presence; to Mireille Harper, Tamsin English, and Rachel Cugnoni, for taking over the reins in editing and cajoling text from me; to Sarah Bennie and Kate Neilan, for brilliant PR and marketing; and to the whole team at Vintage for cheerleading. Pene Parker, thank you once again for your incredible art direction and design, and to David Loftus, for your stunning photography. Rachel, thank you for lending us your beautiful garden and house to work from. Jo Jackson, thank you for your brilliant help on and around the shoot—my food always tastes better when you make it. And Tamsin, you were a legend on shoot!

Grace Helmer, your illustrations are as always so beautiful, I would—and do—have them up on my wall at home, and I'm delighted that you've done such lovely work on this book as with the *Roasting Tin* series.

Pippa Leon and Jo Jackson, thank you both for your considered, thoughtful recipe testing—I very much appreciated having you for second opinions for the book.

To my friends and family, thank you for your love and support, always. Danielle, Emma, Christine, Laura, Rosie, Ruby—what a team to have. Padz, mi hermana (pesce) vegetariana, I hope this book opens lots of interesting new barbecue possibilities for you. Mum and Dad, thank you for lending me the garden to test the book—it was lovely to cook so many dishes for you and get helpful feedback on the recipes and fire-building. (Not sure if Pepper stealing paneer kofte counts as helpful feedback, but it is one of my favorite dishes in the book, so she shows excellent taste—thanks, Principessa.)

INDEX

A

Almonds
  Barbecued sprouts with chili, lemon & almonds 144
  Charred paneer & fennel with chili almonds, lemon & dill 102
  Feta & almond stuffed padrón peppers 42
  Grilled zucchini with Parmesan, almonds & lemon 58
  Orange flower water peaches with rosemary, almonds & cream 206
  Summer pudding packets: vanilla-roasted berries with brioche, mascarpone & almonds 202
Apples
  Dill-drenched feta with beets, cucumber, apple & watercress 104
  Smoked red cabbage with apples, raisins & pecans 140
Apricots: simply roasted apricots with rose & pistachio 196
Artichokes: halloumi with red peppers, artichokes & preserved lemon 52
Arugula: sunshine salad: grilled grapefruit & avocado with arugula & pomegranate 62
Asparagus
  Charred asparagus with chili, peanuts & coconut 28
  Grilled asparagus, radishes & burrata with lemon & basil 48
Avocado 153
  Grapefruit, avocado & pineapple salsa 153
  Mango & avocado salsa 153
  Spiced paneer with mango, avocado, chili & cilantro 106
  Sunshine salad: grilled grapefruit & avocado with arugula & pomegranate 62
  Tomato, & red onion guacamole 153

B

Bananas: the Elvis afternoon barbecue sandwich: chocolate, peanut butter & banana 200
Banh mi 218
Barbecued corn with ginger, peanut & chili dressing 114
Barbecued corn with sage & pine nut butter 120
Barbecued sprouts with chili, lemon & almonds 144
Basil
  Crispy gnocchi—on a skewer—with charred bell peppers & basil pesto 40
  Grilled asparagus, radishes & burrata with lemon & basil 48
  Red pepper, feta, basil & pine nut parcels 170
Beans
  Chipotle mushroom & black bean burgers with peanuts & lime 174
  Grilled feta, pineapple & black bean tacos with chili & lime 108
  Paneer with harissa, green beans, chickpeas & lime 96
  Simple sage & onion cannellini burgers 172

Beans (*continued*)

    Sweet potatoes with rosemary, lemon & black beans 80

    Szechuan eggplant wedges with black bean sauce 178

Beets

    Beet & cumin naan 158

    Dill-drenched feta with beets, cucumber, apple & watercress 104

    Blackberries: Summer pudding packets: vanilla-roasted berries with brioche, mascarpone & almonds 202

Blackened peppers with walnuts, chili & fennel seeds 68

Blue cheese, *see* cheese

Blueberries: Summer pudding packets: vanilla-roasted berries with brioche, mascarpone & almonds 202

Bok choy: five-spice eggplant with bok choy & lime 112

Bread

    Banh mi 218

    Crispy cabbage with chili sage breadcrumbs 146

    Grapefruit & fennel panzanella with honey & watercress 54

    The Elvis afternoon barbecue sandwich: chocolate, peanut butter & banana 200

    Summer pudding packets: vanilla-roasted berries with brioche, mascarpone & almonds 202

    See also flat bread; naan

Breakfast 221

Broccoli

    Charred broccolini with oranges, blue cheese & walnuts 56

    Sesame charred squash with broccolini, spring onions, orange & ginger 88

Brussels sprouts: barbecued sprouts with chili, lemon & almonds 144

Burgers

    Chipotle mushroom & black bean burgers with peanuts & lime 174

    Eggplant & goat cheese burger stacks with honey & thyme 166

    Lime pickle, butternut squash & halloumi burgers 180

    Simple sage & onion cannellini burgers 172

Burrata: grilled asparagus, radishes & burrata with lemon & basil 48

Butternut squash, *see* squash

C

Cabbage

    Crispy cabbage with chili sage breadcrumbs 146

    Smoked red cabbage with apples, raisins & pecans 140

Caramelized mango with smashed cucumber, peanuts & lime 50

Carrots

    Crispy barbecue tofu lettuce wraps with cashews, carrots & nuoc cham 98

    Spiced charred baby carrots with hazelnuts & dill 22

    Squash with charred carrots, red onions, coriander seeds, pistachios & lime 84

Cashews

    Crispy barbecue tofu lettuce wraps with cashews, carrots & nuoc cham 98

    Gunpowder potatoes with fennel seeds, chili, cilantro & cashews 78

    Yuzu mushrooms with cilantro & cashews 130

Cauliflower

    Crispy ginger cauliflower wings with tamarind & cilantro 142

    Jerk cauliflower wings with blue cheese dip 32

Spiced butter cauliflower with marinated feta & lemon 136

Chard: ricotta with grilled squash, chard, honey & hazelnuts 76

Charred asparagus with chili, peanuts & coconut 28

Charred broccolini with oranges, blue cheese & walnuts 56

Charred paneer & fennel with chili almonds, lemon & dill 102

Cheese
    Blue cheese & chive dip 154
    Charred broccolini with oranges, blue cheese & walnuts 56
    Chili cheese French-toasted crumpets with sage 188
    Jerk cauliflower wings with blue cheese dip 32
    Leek & Cheddar Glamorgan sausages 176
    See also burrata; feta; goat cheese; halloumi; mozzarella; paneer; Parmesan; ricotta

Chermoula-dressed sweet potatoes & shallots with pomegranates & mint 86

Cherries, grilled with warm goat cheese, mint & walnuts 26

Chickpeas
    Moroccan grilled potatoes with olives, chickpeas & preserved lemon 90
    Paneer with harissa, green beans, chickpeas & lime 96

Chili
    Barbecued corn with ginger, peanut & chili dressing 114
    Barbecued sprouts with chili, lemon & almonds 144
    Blackened peppers with walnuts, chili & fennel seeds 68
    Charred asparagus with chili, peanuts & coconut 28
    Charred paneer & fennel with chili almonds, lemon & dill 102

Chili cheese French-toasted crumpets with sage 188

Chipotle mushroom & black bean burgers with peanuts & lime 174

Crispy cabbage with chili sage breadcrumbs 146

Eggplant with chili, red onion & cilantro 157

Grilled feta, pineapple & black bean tacos with chili & lime 108

Grilled papaya with tamarind, chili & coconut 60

Gunpowder potatoes with fennel seeds, chili, cilantro & cashews 78

Lime & chili corn fritters with roasted tomatoes 186

Oregano, pine nut & mozzarella-stuffed mushrooms with chili 122

Simply barbecued new potatoes with tarragon, peanuts & chipotle 82

Spiced paneer with mango, avocado, chili & cilantro 106

Chipotle mushroom & black bean burgers with peanuts & lime 174

Chives: blue cheese & chive dip 154

Chocolate
    Dulce de leche passion fruit pots with chocolate & ricotta 204
    The Elvis afternoon barbecue sandwich: chocolate, peanut butter & banana 200

Cilantro
    Chermoula-dressed sweet potatoes & shallots with pomegranate & mint 86
    Chipotle mushroom & black bean burgers with peanut & lime 174
    Crispy ginger cauliflower wings with tamarind & cilantro 142
    Eggplant with chili, red onion & cilantro 157
    Gunpowder potatoes with fennel seeds, chili, cilantro & cashews 78
    Paneer with harissa, green beans, chickpeas & lime 96

Cilantro (*continued*)

Pomegranate & cilantro naan 158

Secret garden whole roasted eggs & new potatoes with salsa verde 190

Spiced paneer kofte with yogurt & cilantro 36

Spiced paneer with mango, avocado, chili & cilantro 106

Sriracha-grilled tofu with pickled onions, lime & cilantro 94

Yuzu mushrooms with cilantro & cashews 130

Cinnamon grilled pineapple with toasted coconut 210

Coconut

Charred asparagus with chili, peanuts & coconut 28

Cinnamon grilled pineapple with toasted coconut 210

Grilled papaya with tamarind, chili & coconut 60

Coriander seeds

Charred Paneer & Fennel with Chili Almonds, Lemon & Dill 102

Garlic, coriander & cumin naan 158

Ricotta with grilled squash, chard, honey & hazelnuts 76

Spiced butter cauliflower with marinated feta & lemon 136

Spiced charred baby carrots with hazelnuts & dill 22

Squash with charred carrots, red onions, coriander seeds, pistachios & lime 84

Thyme-roasted cherry tomatoes with coriander seeds & mozzarella 70

Corn

Barbecued corn with ginger, peanut & chili dressing 114

Barbecued corn with sage & pine nut butter 120

Lime & chili corn fritters with roasted tomatoes 186

Spiced Parmesan corn with lemon & mint 128

Crispy barbecue tofu lettuce wraps with cashews, carrots & nuoc cham 98

Crispy cabbage with chili sage breadcrumbs 146

Crispy ginger cauliflower wings with tamarind & cilantro 142

Crispy gnocchi—on a skewer—with charred bell peppers & basil pesto 40

Crumpets: chili cheese French-toasted crumpets with sage 188

Cucumber

Caramelized mango with smashed cucumber, peanuts & lime 50

Dill-drenched feta with beets, cucumber, apple & watercress 104

Grilled eggplant with cucumber, walnuts & cumin 126

Grilled watermelon with feta, cucumber & mint 34

Cumin

Beet & cumin naan 158

Garlic, coriander & cumin naan 158

Grilled eggplant with cucumber, walnuts & cumin 126

D

Dill

Charred paneer & fennel with chili almonds, lemon & dill 102

Dill-drenched feta with beets, cucumber, apple & watercress 104

Spiced charred baby carrots with hazelnuts & dill 22

Dips

Blue cheese 32

Blue cheese & chive 154

Mint raita 184

Nuoc cham 98

Spring onion & lime 154

Dulce de leche passion fruit pots with chocolate & ricotta 204

E

Eggplant 157
 Eggplant & goat cheese burger stacks with honey & thyme 166
 Eggplant with charred tomatoes & lime 157
 Eggplant with chile, red onion & cilantro 157
 Eggplant with harissa & pomegranate 157
 Five-spice eggplant with bok choy & lime 112
 Grilled eggplant with cucumber, walnuts & cumin 126
 Halloumi-stuffed eggplant with lemon & oregano 132
 Sri Lankan–style eggplant skewers & pickled red onion 64
 Szechuan eggplant wedges with black bean sauce 178
Eggs: secret garden whole roasted eggs & new potatoes with salsa verde 190

F

Fennel
 Charred paneer & fennel with chili almonds, lemon & dill 102
 Grapefruit & fennel panzanella with honey & watercress 54
 Tandoori fennel steaks with mint raita 184
Fennel seeds
 Blackened peppers with walnuts, chili & fennel seeds 68
 Fig, feta & fennel flatbread 161
 Gunpowder potatoes with fennel seeds, chili, cilantro & cashews 78
Feta
 Dill-drenched feta with beets, cucumber, apple & watercress 104
 Feta & almond stuffed padrón peppers 42
 Fig, feta & fennel flatbread 161
 Grilled feta, pineapple & black bean tacos with chili & lime 108
 Grilled watermelon with feta, cucumber & mint 34
 Red pepper, feta, basil & pine nut parcels 170
 Spiced butter cauliflower with marinated feta & lemon 136
Fig, feta & fennel flatbread 161
Five-spice eggplant with bok choy & lime 112
Flatbread
 Fig, feta & fennel flatbread 161
 Pear, ricotta & honey flatbread 161
 Walnut & herb flatbread 161
Fritters, lime & chili corn with roasted tomatoes 186

G

Garlic
 Garlic, coriander & cumin naan 158
 Roasted garlic tzatziki 154
Ginger
 Barbecued corn with ginger, peanut & chili dressing 114
 Sesame charred squash with broccolini, spring onions, orange & ginger 88
Glamorgan sausages, leek & Cheddar 176
Gnocchi: Crispy gnocchi—on a skewer—with charred bell peppers & basil pesto 40
Goat cheese
 Eggplant & goat cheese burger stacks with honey & thyme 166
 Grilled cherries with warm goat cheese, mint & walnuts 26
Grapefruit
 Grapefruit & fennel panzanella with honey & watercress 54
 Grapefruit, avocado & pineapple salsa 153
 Sunshine salad: grilled grapefruit & avocado with arugula & pomegranate 62
Grilled asparagus, radishes & burrata with lemon & basil 48

Grilled cherries with warm goat cheese, mint & walnuts 26

Grilled eggplant with cucumber, walnuts & cumin 126

Grilled feta, pineapple & black bean tacos with chili & lime 108

Grilled papaya with tamarind, chili & coconut 60

Grilled pineapple, halloumi & mint skewers 30

Grilled portobello mushrooms & leeks with tarragon & walnuts 118

Grilled watermelon with feta, cucumber & mint 34

Grilled zucchini with Parmesan, almonds & lemon 58

Guacamole, tomato, & red onion 153

Gunpowder potatoes with fennel seeds, chili, cilantro & cashews 78

H

Halloumi

Grilled pineapple, halloumi & mint skewers 30

Halloumi-stuffed eggplant with lemon & oregano 132

Halloumi with red peppers, artichokes & preserved lemon 52

Lime pickle, butternut squash & halloumi burgers 180

Rosemary grilled mushrooms with crispy halloumi & lemon 20

Harissa

Eggplant with harissa & pomegranate 157

Paneer with harissa, green beans, chickpeas & lime 96

Hazelnuts

Ricotta with grilled squash, chard, honey & hazelnuts 76

Spiced charred baby carrots with hazelnuts & dill 22

Honey

Eggplant & goat cheese burger stacks with honey & thyme 166

Grapefruit & fennel panzanella with honey & watercress 54

Honey & orange grilled papaya with mint 212

Pear, ricotta & honey flatbread 161

Ricotta with grilled squash, chard, honey & hazelnuts 76

J

Jerk cauliflower wings with blue cheese dip 32

K

Kofte: spiced paneer kofte with yogurt & cilantro 36

L

Leeks

Grilled portobello mushrooms & leeks with tarragon & walnuts 118

Leek & Cheddar Glamorgan sausages 176

Lemon

Barbecued sprouts with chili, lemon & almonds 144

Charred paneer & fennel with chili almonds, lemon & dill 102

Grilled asparagus, radishes & burrata with lemon & basil 48

Grilled zucchini with Parmesan, almonds & lemon 58

Halloumi-stuffed eggplant with lemon & oregano 132

Halloumi with red peppers, artichokes & preserved lemon 52

Moroccan grilled potatoes with olives, chickpeas & preserved lemon 90

Lemon (*continued*)

Rosemary grilled mushrooms with crispy halloumi & lemon 20

Spiced butter cauliflower with marinated feta & lemon 136

Spiced Parmesan corn with lemon & mint 128

Sweet potatoes with rosemary, lemon & black beans 80

Lime

Caramelized mango with smashed cucumber, peanuts & lime 50

Chipotle mushroom & black bean burgers with peanuts & lime 174

Eggplant with charred tomatoes & lime 157

Five-spice eggplant with bok choy & lime 112

Grilled feta, pineapple & black bean tacos with chili & lime 108

Lime & chili corn fritters with roasted tomatoes 186

Lime pickle, butternut squash & halloumi burgers 180

Paneer with harissa, green beans, chickpeas & lime 96

Spring onion & lime dip 154

Squash with charred carrots, red onions, coriander seeds, pistachios & lime 84

Sriracha-grilled tofu with pickled onions, lime & cilantro 94

Mint

Chermoula-dressed sweet potatoes & shallots with pomegranates & mint 86

Grilled cherries with warm goat cheese, mint & walnuts 26

Grilled pineapple, halloumi & mint skewers 30

Grilled watermelon with feta, cucumber & mint 34

Honey & orange grilled papaya with mint 212

Spiced Parmesan corn with lemon & mint 128

Tandoori fennel steaks with mint raita 184

Moroccan grilled potatoes with olives, chickpeas & preserved lemon 90

Mozzarella

Oregano, pine nut & mozzarella-stuffed mushrooms with chili 122

Thyme-roasted cherry tomatoes with coriander seeds & mozzarella 70

Mushrooms

Chipotle mushroom & black bean burgers with peanuts & lime 174

Grilled portobello mushrooms & leeks with tarragon & walnuts 118

Oregano, pine nut & mozzarella-stuffed mushrooms with chili 122

Rosemary grilled mushrooms with crispy halloumi & lemon 20

Yuzu mushrooms with cilantro & cashews 130

M

Mango

Caramelized mango with smashed cucumber, peanuts & lime 50

Mango & avocado salsa 153

Spiced paneer with mango, avocado, chili & cilantro 106

Mascarpone: Summer pudding packets: vanilla-roasted berries with brioche, mascarpone & almonds 202

N

Naan

Beet & cumin naan 158

Garlic, coriander & cumin naan 158

Pomegranate & cilantro naan 158

Noodle bowl 219

Nuoc cham 98

Nuts, *see* almonds; cashews; hazelnuts; peanuts; pecans; pine nuts; pistachios; walnuts

O

Olives: Moroccan grilled potatoes with olives, chickpeas & preserved lemon 90

Onions
Eggplant with chili, red onion & cilantro 157
Sesame charred squash with broccolini, spring onions, orange & ginger 88
Simple sage & onion cannellini burgers 172
Spring onion & lime dip 154
Squash with charred carrots, red onions, coriander seeds, pistachios & lime 84
Sri Lankan–style eggplant skewers & pickled red onion 64
Sriracha-grilled tofu with pickled onions, lime & cilantro 94
Tomato, & red onion guacamole 153
Vietnamese grilled tofu with tomatoes & spring onions 100

Orange
Charred broccolini with oranges, blue cheese & walnuts 56
Honey & orange grilled papaya with mint 212
Sesame charred squash with broccolini, spring onions, orange & ginger 88
Orange flower water peaches with rosemary, almonds & cream 206

Oregano
Halloumi-stuffed eggplant with lemon & oregano 132
Oregano, pine nut & mozzarella-stuffed mushrooms with chili 122

P

Paneer
Charred paneer & fennel with chili almonds, lemon & dill 102
Paneer with harissa, green beans, chickpeas & lime 96
Spiced paneer kofte with yogurt & cilantro 36
Spiced paneer with mango, avocado, chili & cilantro 106

Panzanella: grapefruit & fennel panzanella with honey & watercress 54

Papaya
Grilled papaya with tamarind, chili & coconut 60
Honey & orange grilled papaya with mint 212

Parcels, red pepper, feta, basil & pine nut 170

Parmesan
Grilled zucchini with Parmesan, almonds & lemon 58
Spiced Parmesan corn with lemon & mint 128

Passion fruit: dulce de leche passion fruit pots with chocolate & ricotta 204

Pasta 220

Peaches: orange flower water peaches with rosemary, almonds & cream 206

Peanuts
Barbecued corn with ginger, peanut & chili dressing 114
Caramelized mango with smashed cucumber, peanuts & lime 50
Charred asparagus with chili, peanuts & coconut 28
Chipotle mushroom & black bean burgers with peanuts & lime 174
Simply barbecued new potatoes with tarragon, peanuts & chipotle 82
The Elvis afternoon barbecue sandwich: chocolate, peanut butter & banana 200

Pears
Pear, ricotta & honey flatbread 161
Saffron pears & rhubarb with ricotta 198

Pecans: smoked red cabbage with apples, raisins & pecans 140

Peppers
Blackened peppers with walnuts, chili & fennel seeds 68
Crispy gnocchi—on a skewer—with charred bell peppers & basil pesto 40

Peppers (*continued*)
Feta & almond stuffed padrón peppers 42
Halloumi with red peppers, artichokes &
preserved lemon 52
Red pepper, feta, basil & pine nut parcels 170
Pesto
Basil 40
Walnut 68
Pineapple
Cinnamon grilled pineapple with toasted
coconut 210
Grapefruit, avocado & pineapple salsa 153
Grilled feta, pineapple & black bean tacos
with chili & lime 108
Grilled pineapple, halloumi & mint skewers
30
Pine nuts
Barbecued corn with sage & pine nut
butter 120
Oregano, pine nut & mozzarella-stuffed
mushrooms with chili 122
Red pepper, feta, basil & pine nut parcels 170
Pistachios
Simply roasted apricots with rose &
pistachio 196
Squash with charred carrots, red onions,
coriander seeds, pistachios & lime 84
Pomegranates
Chermoula-dressed sweet potatoes &
shallots with pomegranates & mint 86
Eggplant with harissa & pomegranate 157
Pomegranate & cilantro naan 158
Sunshine salad: grilled grapefruit & avocado
with arugula & pomegranate 62
Potatoes
Gunpowder potatoes with fennel seeds,
chili, cilantro & cashews 78
Moroccan grilled potatoes with olives,
chickpeas & preserved lemon 90
Secret garden whole roasted eggs & new
potatoes with salsa verde 190
Simple sage & onion cannellini burgers 172

Simply barbecued new potatoes with
tarragon, peanuts & chipotle 82
See also sweet potatoes

R

Radishes: grilled asparagus, radishes &
burrata with lemon & basil 48
Raspberries: Summer pudding packets:
vanilla-roasted berries with brioche,
mascarpone & almonds 202
Red pepper, feta, basil & pine nut parcels 170
Rhubarb: saffron pears & rhubarb with ricotta
198
Rice bowl 219
Ricotta
Dulce de leche passion fruit pots with
chocolate & ricotta 204
Pear, ricotta & honey flatbread 161
Ricotta with grilled squash, chard, honey &
hazelnuts 76
Saffron pears & rhubarb with ricotta 198
Roasted garlic tzatziki 154
Rosemary
Rosemary grilled mushrooms with crispy
halloumi & lemon 20
Sweet potatoes with rosemary, lemon &
black beans 80
Rosewater: simply roasted apricots with rose
& pistachio 196

S

Saffron pears & rhubarb with ricotta 198
Sage
Barbecued corn with sage & pine nut
butter 120
Chili cheese French-toasted crumpets
with sage 188
Crispy cabbage with chili sage
breadcrumbs 146
Simple sage & onion cannellini burgers 172

Salads
Chopped salads 150
Grapefruit & fennel panzanella with honey & watercress 54
Grated salads 150
Grilled asparagus, radishes & burrata with lemon & basil 48
How to make 148–149
Potato salads 150
Ribbon salads 150
Shredded salads 150
Sunshine salad: grilled grapefruit & avocado with arugula & pomegranate 62
Salsa
Grapefruit, avocado & pineapple salsa 153
Mango & avocado salsa 153
Salsa verde 190
Secret garden whole roasted eggs & new potatoes with salsa verde 190
Sesame charred squash with broccolini, spring onions, orange & ginger 88
Shallots: chermoula-dressed sweet potatoes & shallots with pomegranates & mint 86
Simple sage & onion cannellini burgers 172
Simply barbecued new potatoes with tarragon, peanuts & chipotle 82
Simply roasted apricots with rose & pistachio 196
Skewers
Crispy gnocchi—on a skewer—with charred bell peppers & basil pesto 40
Grilled pineapple, halloumi & mint skewers 30
Rosemary grilled mushrooms with crispy halloumi & lemon 20
Sri Lankan–style eggplant skewers & pickled red onion 64
Smoked red cabbage with apples, raisins & pecans 140
Sour cream 154
Blue cheese & chive dip 154
Roasted garlic tzatziki 154
Spring onion & lime dip 154

Spiced butter cauliflower with marinated feta & lemon 136
Spiced charred baby carrots with hazelnuts & dill 22
Spiced paneer kofte with yogurt & cilantro 36
Spiced paneer with mango, avocado, chili & cilantro 106
Spiced Parmesan corn with lemon & mint 128
Spring onion & lime dip 154
Squash
Lime pickle, butternut squash & halloumi burgers 180
Ricotta with grilled squash, chard, honey & hazelnuts 76
Sesame charred squash with broccolini, spring onions, orange & ginger 88
Squash with charred carrots, red onions, coriander seeds, pistachios & lime 84
Sri Lankan–style eggplant skewers & pickled red onion 64
Sriracha-grilled tofu with pickled onions, lime & cilantro 94
Summer pudding packets: vanilla-roasted berries with brioche, mascarpone & almonds 202
Sunshine salad: grilled grapefruit & avocado with arugula & pomegranate 62
Sweet potatoes
Chermoula-dressed sweet potatoes & shallots with pomegranates & mint 86
Sweet potatoes with rosemary, lemon & black beans 80
Szechuan eggplant wedges with black bean sauce 178

T

Tacos: grilled feta, pineapple & black bean tacos with chili & lime 108
Tamarind
Crispy ginger cauliflower wings with tamarind & cilantro 142

Tamarind (*continued*)

Grilled papaya with tamarind, chili & coconut 60

Tandoori fennel steaks with mint raita 184

Tarragon

Grilled portobello mushrooms & leeks with tarragon & walnuts 118

Simply barbecued new potatoes with tarragon, peanuts & chipotle 82

The Elvis afternoon barbecue sandwich: chocolate, peanut butter & banana 200

Thyme

Eggplant & goat cheese burger stacks with honey & thyme 166

Thyme-roasted cherry tomatoes with coriander seeds & mozzarella 70

Tofu

Crispy barbecue tofu lettuce wraps with cashews, carrots & nuoc cham 98

Sriracha-grilled tofu with pickled onions, lime & cilantro 94

Vietnamese grilled tofu with tomatoes & spring onions 100

Tomatoes

Eggplant with charred tomatoes & lime 157

Lime & chili corn fritters with roasted tomatoes 186

Thyme-roasted cherry tomatoes with coriander seeds & mozzarella 70

Tomato, & red onion guacamole 153

Vietnamese grilled tofu with tomatoes & spring onions 100

Tzatziki, roasted garlic 154

V

Vanilla-roasted berries with brioche, mascarpone & almonds, summer pudding packets 202

Vietnamese grilled tofu with tomatoes & spring onions 100

W

Walnuts

Blackened peppers with walnuts, chili & fennel seeds 68

Charred broccolini with oranges, blue cheese & walnuts 56

Grilled cherries with warm goat cheese, mint & walnuts 26

Grilled eggplant with cucumber, walnuts & cumin 126

Grilled portobello mushrooms & leeks with tarragon & walnuts 118

Walnut & herb flatbread 161

Watercress

Dill-drenched feta with beets, cucumber, apple & watercress 104

Grapefruit & fennel panzanella with honey & watercress 54

Watermelon, grilled with feta, cucumber & mint 34

Y

Yogurt

Spiced paneer kofte with yogurt & cilantro 36

Tandoori fennel steaks with mint raita 184

Yuzu mushrooms with cilantro & cashews 130

Z

Zucchini: grilled with Parmesan, almonds & lemon 58

ABOUT THE AUTHOR

Rukmini Iyer is the best-selling author of the *Roasting Tin* series. She is a recipe writer, food stylist, and formerly a lawyer. She loves creating delicious and easy recipes with minimum fuss and maximum flavor. Rukmini believes family dinners are an integral part of the day and is passionate about helping people make it possible.

Rukmini grew up in Cambridgeshire, England, with the best of three food cultures: Bengali and South Indian food from her parents' Indian heritage, along with classic '80s mac & cheese, sponge puddings, and cheese & pineapple on skewers. Rukmini's career began with a training contract at a leading law firm, but she realized that, as she spent all day thinking about food, all evening cooking, and most of her law lectures or time in the office scribbling down ideas for new dishes in the margins of her notebook, a career in food was a sensible move. She decided to retrain as a food stylist, so after cooking school and a summer working at a Michelin-starred restaurant to learn the ropes, she began work as a food stylist. Surrounded by food all day on photo shoots, she noticed the meals she made at home grew simpler, often just in a roasting pan, and that there were ways of packing flavor and interest into the dishes with an absolute minimum effort—this became the inspiration for the series.

As well as writing cookbooks, Rukmini styles and writes recipes for numerous brands and publications, including Waitrose, the *Guardian,* and Fortnum & Mason. When not working with food, she can usually be found walking her beautiful border collie, Pepper, by the riverside in East London, entertaining at home, or filling her balcony and flat with more plants than they can hold. Rukmini runs an occasional series of supper clubs for charities, including Oxfam and Women's Aid.

 @ missminifer   @ missminifer

First published as *The Green Barbecue* in 2021 by Square Peg, an imprint of Vintage.
Vintage is part of the Penguin Random House group of companies.

For information about permission to reproduce selections from this book, write to
Permissions, Countryman Press, 500 Fifth Avenue, New York, NY 10110

For information about special discounts for bulk purchases, please contact
W. W. Norton Special Sales at specialsales@wwnorton.com or 800-233-4830

Manufacturing by Versa Press
Production manager: Devon Zahn

Countryman Press
www.countrymanpress.com

An imprint of W. W. Norton & Company, Inc.
500 Fifth Avenue, New York, NY 10110
www.wwnorton.com

978-1-68268-749-9 (pbk.)

10 9 8 7 6 5 4 3 2 1